# A Capital Guide for Kids

Vanessa Miles comes from a famous theatrical family – her brother
Christopher is a film director, her sister Sarah is an actress – and
before the birth of her son she was herself a successful actress,
appearing in many stage and television productions. She began
broadcasting with Capital Radio in 1978, presenting her "Junior
What's On" spot on the Michael Aspel Show. It proved so popular
and so helpful that she decided to incorporate her researches into
this book. Her other broadcasting activities currently include reading children's stories on television, "Listen With Mother" on BBC
Radio 4, and book discussions and interviews on "Alternatives",
Capital Radio's arts programme.

# A
# Capital Guide for
# Kids

A
London guide for parents with small
children

by
VANESSA MILES

Allison & Busby
London

First published in Great Britain 1982
by Allison and Busby Limited
6a Noel Street, London W1V 3RB

Copyright © Vanessa Miles 1982

British Library Cataloguing in Publication Data:

Miles, Vanessa
    A capital guide for kids.
    1.  London—Description and travel—1951—
    Guide-books—Juvenile literature
    I.  Title
    914.21'04858        DA679

    ISBN 0-85031-441-0
    ISBN 0-85031-438-0        Pbk

Set in 10/11 pt Imprint by Alan Sutton Publishers
and printed in Great Britain by
Richard Clay, Bungay, Suffolk.

# CONTENTS

## To Luke With Love

My thanks to Jacqueline Danks without whose continual help and encouragement this book would never have been completed.

# FOREWORD

Vanessa Miles's enthusiasm makes Tigger seem like an old stick-in-the-mud. Her broadcasts on Capital Radio register high on the Richter scale, as she joyfully presents her "What's on for small people". Any mother of an under-five who still complains of being bored simply hasn't been listening.

The phone calls that follow Vanessa's broadcasts keep our information staff busy, and they, as much as any frantic parent, will be delighted that she has compiled this guide. As you will see, it is all-embracing in its range. You will find things to do and places to go, whether for fun or for relief (see p. 98).

In her research, Vanessa Miles has lived up to her name and travelled great distances. If she were paid by the mile, she would be a rich woman. She has certainly enriched the life of her small son, the listeners to our programme, and now the readers of her book. Buy two – one for your own shelf, and another for someone you really like.

MICHAEL ASPEL

# INTRODUCTION

The intention of this book is to provide parents with a comprehensive guide to London for their pre-school children. As a broadcaster on the Michael Aspel show for Capital Radio, I realized what an enormous demand there was for a central source of information where parents could quickly and easily find out what was available in London for small children. The parents I met and the many people who telephoned and wrote in asking for more details of current events, were all keen to find out new ways of entertaining their offspring. Under-fives who were not at school full-time were a particular problem. What could they do when not at playgroup or nursery?

I decided to turn detective and set off with my three-year-old in tow to try and find out exactly what was going on in town. We combed London boroughs and were often surprised by what we found – but rarely disappointed. I soon realized that a child's capacity for learning, for adapting and for sheer enjoyment is boundless. We discovered such things as toy libraries, museums with special sections for fives and under, magic shows, sports centres, concerts and a myriad of other activities and entertainments.

I hope you enjoy them all as much as we did.

To the best of my knowledge the information in this book is correct at the time of going press – but do let me know if I have omitted anything.

V.M.

# 1

# Around and About

## ENTERTAINMENT

There is a wide variety of theatrical activity specializing in producing entertainment for 5s and under. These include puppet and magic shows, plays, films and concerts.

All children, even the smallest toddlers, can appreciate and enjoy live theatre, and it is easy to forget how good their powers of concentration can be at this age. The success of the ever-increasing number of children's theatres proves their value and meets the obvious growing demand for entertainment for the pre-school child.

## Theatres

**Bubble Theatre Company,**
9 Kingsford Street, NW5. Tel: 01-485 3420.
The Bubble is Britain's only fully mobile theatre. Performing in its gaily coloured "bubble" tent, it tours the parks, greens and commons of Greater London throughout the summer. The Company performs a variety of plays aimed at different age groups. For venues, dates and time of performances, ring the Company direct.

**Common Stock Theatre,**
31 Fulham Palace Road, W6. Tel: 01-741 3086.
Common Stock is a professional community theatre based in Hammersmith. Their aim is to bring live entertainment to people who don't normally go to the theatre and they perform in a large number of venues throughout the Greater London area. There are usually a couple of plays in the repertoire suitable for children and touring dates are between April and November. For further information on programmes and touring dates ring the company direct.

**Croydon Warehouse,**
62 Dingwall Road, Croydon. Tel: 01-680 4060.
Regular Saturday morning shows take place at 11.00 am. Telephone for details of their current production.
*British Rail:*   East Croydon.

**Little Angel Marionette Theatre,**
Dagmar Passage, Cross Street, Islington, N1. Tel: 01-226 1787.
This is one of the few permanent puppet theatres which provide regular Saturday morning entertainment for children. Performances for under-5s begin at 11.00 am and last for approximately 50 minutes with an interval halfway through when orange and biscuits are on sale in the foyer. The selection of exotic and colourful puppets have made this a very popular little theatre, so it's advisable to book in advance.
*Tube:*   Angel.
*Bus:*     4, 19, 30, 43, 104, 172, 279 to Upper Street; 38, 73, 171, 277 to Essex Road.

**Lyric Theatre,**
King Street, Hammersmith, W6. Tel: 01-741 2311.
The Lyric specializes in a variety of entertainments including clowns, puppets and short plays, which take place on Saturday mornings in the upstairs theatre studio. Check beforehand that the current production is suitable for your child's age group.
*Tube:*   Hammersmith.
*Bus:*     9, 11, 27, 33, 72, 73, 91, 220, 260, 266, 267, 290.

**Movingstage Marionettes,**
Theatre Barge, Camden Lock, Commercial Place, NW1. Tel: 01-249 6876.
The company have converted the old Thames barge into a floating

theatre and from September until Easter are moored at Camden Lock. During the summer months they tour the canals, performing at different venues en route. Under-5s are entertained on Sundays at noon. Telephone for details of their summer schedule.
*Tube:* Chalk Farm.
*Bus:* 24, 31, 68.

**Nomad Puppets,**
8 Kingly Street, W1. Tel: 01-437 5396; weekends: 01-767 4005.
Ideal for a first-time visit, this miniature theatre which seats thirty is run by a family of puppeteers who create a very friendly and informal atmosphere. They give two shows at weekends. On Saturday, there is "a puppet party show", with games, prizes and tea, when you can leave your child if you wish. On Sunday there is a slightly shorter show.
*Tube:* Oxford Circus, Piccadilly Circus.
*Bus:* 3, 6, 12, 13, 15, 39, 53, 59, 88, 159 to Regent Street.

**Polka Children's Theatre,**
240 The Broadway, Wimbledon, SW19. Tel: 01-542 4258.
A resident theatre company with high-quality productions of mime, magic and music. The Polka Centre also houses a permanent museum of puppets and toys, a playground, an adventure room and a café, designed especially for children, called The Pantry.
*Tube:* Wimbledon.
*Bus:* 57, 93, 131, 155, 293.

**Riverside Studios,**
Crisp Road, Hammersmith, W6. Tel: 01-748 3354.
There is always something happening here at weekends, especially during the holidays. Entertainments range from jugglers to Punch and Judy shows, short films and cartoons. They also have a self-service snack bar and a good bookshop.
*Tube:* Hammersmith.
*Bus:* 9, 27, 33, 72, 73, 91, 267, 290.

**Roundhouse,**
Chalk Farm Road, NW1. Tel: 01-267 2541.
The Roundhouse puts on regular Saturday matinées for children of all ages, including 5s and under. In the repertoire are a variety of plays and puppet shows.
*Tube:* Chalk Farm.
*Bus:* 24, 31, 68.

**Tricycle Theatre,**
269 Kilburn High Road, NW6. Tel: 01-328 8626.
The Tricycle Theatre puts on Saturday afternoon children's shows
at 2.30 pm, and there is usually something suitable for 5s and
under.
*Tube:* Kilburn.
*Bus:* 8, 16, 32, 176, 616.

**Unicorn Theatre for Young People,**
Great Newport Street, WC2. Tel: 01-836 3334.
At weekends and during the school holidays, 4- to 7-year-olds are
entertained in the Unicorn's studio upstairs. Plays are com-
missioned especially for this age group and the standard of writing
is extremely high. The Unicorn also has a theatre club, where for a
small membership charge you can join in the various theatre
workshops, again run at weekends and during the holidays. For
further details of membership and future programmes telephone:
01-240 2076.
*Tube:* Leicester Square.
*Bus:* 1, 24, 29, 176.

**Upstream Children's Theatre,**
St Andrew's Church, Short Street, SE1. Tel: 01-633 9819.
The Upstream Children's Theatre has been in existence since 1978,
and has recently become a full-time project with actor teachers.
While their main aim is to introduce and involve children in general
theatre through their workshops, they also put on occasional plays
for young children.
*Tube:* Waterloo.
*Bus:* 1, 4, 68, 70, 76, 176, 188, 239, 501, 502, 513.

## Theatre in the Parks

There are free shows plus many other events in the London parks.
Each year the programme includes puppet and magic shows put on
by touring theatre groups and open-air music. The GLC Parks
Department has a comprehensive leaflet giving details. Tel: 01-
633 1707.

For other local events such as fairs, circuses and fêtes ring your
local borough council's entertainment department.

# Music
## Family Concerts at Morley College,
61 Westminster Bridge Road, SE1. Tel: 01-928 8501.
A chance for the whole family, once a month, to work together
with music. You can listen to, or join in with everything from
opera and jazz to steel bands and suzuki violins. Relaxed, informal
and fun but most important you don't have to be musical to join in
– just enjoy the music.
*Tube:* Lambeth North or Waterloo Station (SR), then a ten-
minute walk to the college.
*Bus:* 12, 53, 171, 184.
## Purcell Room,
South Bank, SE1. Tel: 01-928 3191.
Throughout the year the Purcell Room holds special mini concerts
for children. They take place once or twice a month on Sunday
afternoons when 5-year-olds and over are entertained by music and
story-telling. For dates and programme details telephone direct.
*Tube:* Waterloo.
*Bus:* 1, 4, 55, 68, 70, 76, 149, 168a, 171, 176, 188, 239, 501,
502, 507, 513.

# Cinemas
## Institute of Contemporary Arts (ICA),
Nash House, The Mall, SW1. Tel: 01-930 6393.
When you buy a ticket to the ICA's children's cinema show, you
automatically get free membership to their club. There are regular
Saturday and Sunday afternoon programmes, including cartoons
and adventure stories. Check before you go to find out what films
are currently showing.
*Tube:* Trafalgar Square.
*Bus:* 1, 1a, 3, 6, 9, 9a, 11, 12, 13, 15, 24, 29, 39, 53, 59, 77,
77a, 77c, 88, 159, 168, 170, 176.
## Rio Centre,
107 Kingsland High Street, E8. Tel: 01-254 6677.
Double bills of children's films and cartoons are put on during the
school holidays and half-term, with a programme change each
week. Check for details.
*Tube:* Highbury & Islington.
*Bus:* 67, 76, 97, 149, 236, 243.

# Fun and Leisure Centres

There are a number of centres for young children in the London area that provide exciting backgrounds against which they can act out their own games and stories in a safe environment. Some also provide facilities for making things, painting and generally learning through play.

**Action Space Soft Room,**
Drill Hall, 16 Chenies Street, WC1. Tel: 01-637 8270.
Especially for 5s and under, Action Space Soft Room comprises a "soft" environment of inflatables and foam mats, and the sessions are structured like an animated story-telling with the Action Space team as the characters in the story. Sessions are usually held on Tuesdays, and a course lasts from 4 to 6 weeks. The group also arranges visits to local playgroups. For further information telephone 01-637 8270 and ask for Caroline Bagnell or Peter Shelton.
*Tube:* Goodge Street.
*Bus:* 14, 24, 29, 73, 176.

**Battersea Arts Centre,**
Old Town Hall, Lavender Hill, SW11. Tel: 01-223 8413.
The Centre is run specifically for children of all ages and provides facilities for a wide variety of different activities some of which are suitable for 5s and under. Included in their programme is a Sunday morning family pottery workshop at 11.00 where everyone can try their hand at making something out of clay. Additional classes and other activities are put on during the school holidays.
*British Rail:* Clapham Junction from Victoria.
*Bus:* 45, 77, 77a, 168.

**Children's Drama Workshop,**
Earl's Court Youth Club, 120 Ifield Road, SW10. Tel: 01-373 3299.
Every Saturday June Abbott holds her drama and improvisation classes for children. Not suitable for the very tiny, they are nevertheless ideal for extrovert 4+s and 5-year-olds. For more information ring her at the above number.
*Tube:* Earl's Court.
*Bus:* 31, 74.

**Family Saturday Arts Centre,**
Camden Institute, Holmes Road, NW5. Tel: 01-267 1414.
From September to April the Camden Institute holds a Family

Arts Centre every Saturday during term time. Parents and children can work together in the different workshops and the atmosphere is relaxed and informal. Teachers are on hand to give help and advice if needed. If you are interested in finding out more, go and have a look round without obligation: they will be pleased to show you what is going on. Enrolment is for a term.

*Tube:* Kentish Town.

*Bus:* 27, 134, 137, 214 and 46 to Prince of Wales Road.

**Upstream Children's Theatre,**

St Andrew's Church, Short Street, SE1. Tel: 01-633 9819.

The drama workshops run here are suitable for children of 4 years-old upwards and aim at exploring the magic of theatre through games, improvisations and performances. Sessions take place on Saturdays, 10.00 am–12.00 noon and 1.00–3.00 pm.

*Tube:* Waterloo.

*Bus:* 1, 4, 6, 68, 70, 76, 176, 188, 239, 501, 502, 513.

## Other Community Centres

**Dalston Children's Centre,**

9a (basement) Sandringham Road, E8. Tel: 01-254 9661.

A community-based project, the Dalston Children's Centre is negotiating with the local council to move into a new "children's house". In the meantime they are already operating a "drop-in" and organizing some special activities for under-5s, such as dance classes and a theatre season. Telephone for details.

*British Rail:* Dalston Junction.

*Bus:* 30, 38, 48, 67, 76, 149, 243, 277.

**Jackson's Lane Community Centre,**

Archway Road, N6. Tel: 01-340 5226.

The Mother and Toddler Club is open on Mondays, Wednesdays and Fridays. The Centre also puts on occasional shows for children – telephone for details.

*Tube:* Highgate.

*Bus:* 43, 104, 134, 210, 263.

**Under-5s at 46 Longridge Road,**

SW5. Tel: 01-370 6030.

For those living in the vicinity of Earl's Court this is a "drop-in"

centre open each weekday 10.00 am–12.30 pm and 2.00–4.30 pm.
There is a supervisor in charge but parents must stay throughout.
*Tube:*  Earl's Court.
*Bus:*  31, 74.

For up-to-date details of current seasonal entertainment for
children, look in one of the weekly London listings magazines such
as *City Limits* or *Time Out*.

# 2

# Expeditions and Rambles

People rarely bother to visit and enjoy the sights of interest in their own home town and so miss out on the pleasure of discovering new places near at hand. Exploring is usually reserved for holidays and the effort needed to organize a day out seems much greater when sitting at home among the household chores. But London is one of the most interesting capitals in the world – so why not be a tourist for a day?

## RIVERS AND CANALS

All major cities rely on water for their existence, London is no exception and one of the best ways to spend a day out in the city is to take one of the many river and canal trips which run from April to October.

### River Trips

The only way to see the kaleidoscope of fascinating things the Thames has to offer is actually on the river itself. And when you go, why not take a picnic along too? Don't forget to wrap up well; it can be chilly aboard, even on a summer day.

21

All the boat trips listed below leave from Westminster Pier (opposite Big Ben).

*Tube:*    Westminster.

*Bus:*     3, 11, 12, 24, 29, 53, 70, 76, 77, 88, 109, 155, 159, 168, 170, 172, 184, 503.

During the summer months only (April–October), pleasure launches leave Westminster Pier on a round-trip sightseeing cruise every 45 minutes, from 11.30 am to 5.00 pm, and the trip lasts an hour. For further details telephone 01-839 4859.

## Down the River

Pleasure launches leave for the Tower of London and Greenwich every 20 minutes, from 10.00 am. During the winter the trips are every 30 minutes. For more details telephone 01-930 4097/1616.

## Up the River

During the summer from 10.30 am to 3.30 pm, boats leave for Kew every 30 minutes. There is also a day trip to Hampton Court, calling in at Richmond. For more information telephone 01-930 2074/2026.

## Boats on the River

There are many exciting boats to see on the river at any time of the year. Here are a few that you can board.

**Cutty Sark,**

Greenwich Pier, SW10.

Open Monday to Saturday 11.00 am–6.00 pm (closes at 5.00 pm in the winter); Sunday 2.30–6.00 pm (5.00 pm in winter).

The famous tea-clipper *Cutty Sark*, which in its day was one of the fastest vessels travelling the Far East run with its fine cargoes of tea, lies just a stone's throw away from Greenwich Pier. It is now a museum and down in her bows are a selection of fine figureheads. On deck you can view the tiny galley and crew's quarters.

*British Rail:*    Maze Hill.

*Bus:*     53, 54, 75, 177, 180, 185.

**Gypsy Moth** is moored close by the *Cutty Sark*, and has the same opening times winter and summer. Sir Francis Chichester sailed round the world in this small boat which appears far too fragile for such a long and arduous journey.

Nearest station and buses as above.

## The Historic Ships Collection,

Maritime Trust, 52 St Katharine's Dock, St Katharine's Way, E1.
Tel: 01-481 0043.
Open daily 10.00 am–5.00 pm (July and August 10.00 am–7.00 pm).

Moored along the East Basin of St Katharine's Dock is the Maritime Trust's Historic Ships Collection. It comprises six different vessels including a tug, a sailing barge and the famous R.R.S. *Discovery*, in which Captain Scott made his remarkable voyage to the Antarctic. You can go on board and explore below deck and find out how these lovely old ships operated.
*Tube:* Aldgate, Tower Hill.
*Bus:* 9, 42, 67, 78.

# Canal Trips

After years of disuse and decline, the canals have now come into their own again, but with a strong emphasis on leisure, not industry. Chugging along at a leisurely five miles an hour past colourful houseboats and water-birds, you get an unusual glimpse of London. During the summer months, April to October, trips to take are:

## Porta Bella Packet,

Ladbroke Grove and Kensal Road, W10. Tel: 01-960 5456.
This takes you up through Paddington to Little Venice and Browning Island (named after the poet who lived there for some years), past the zoo and under Lord Snowdon's aviary and on to the Cumberland Basin and back again. The return trip takes just under two hours, but if this seems too long, you can get off at the zoo. Again, it might be a good idea to take a picnic along.
*Tube:* Ladbroke Grove.
*Bus:* 15, 295.

## Jason's Boat Trip,

(opposite no. 60) Blomfield Road, W9. Tel: 01-286 3428.
Towing a "narrow boat" behind her, the *Jason* goes up through Regent's Park to Camden Lock and back again. The return journey takes about two hours, and trips run from April to October at 2.00 and 4.00 pm with an extra 11.00 am trip in June, July and August.
*Tube:* Warwick Avenue.
*Bus:* 6, 16.

**Jenny Wren,**
Garden Jetty, Camden Lock, Commercial Place, Chalk Farm
Road, NW1. Tel: 01-485 4433.
This is a much shorter trip going from Camden Lock to Little
Venice and back. The return journey takes roughly an hour. The
*Jenny Wren* operates from April to October. For more details
phone the office, as departures times vary.
*Tube:*  Camden Town.
*Bus:*    24, 31, 68.
**Zoo Waterbus,**
Canal Office, Delamere Terrace, W2. Tel: 01-286 6101.
This regular service to and from the Zoo (April–October) is an
exciting way of getting there as well as another means of exploring
London's waterways. (Further details of waterbus p. 28).
*Tube:*  Warwick Avenue.
*Bus:*    6, 16.

# SIGHTSEEING SPECIALS

Small children get tired easily and it is often difficult to hold their attention for any length of time. Although many of London's well-known tourist attractions are not considered suitable for the very young, the selection below has a special appeal for all ages.

## Changing the Guard,
Buckingham Palace, The Mall, SW1.

This takes place in the Palace forecourt every morning at 11.30 am, weather permitting, from April to September and on alternate days in winter. The Guards, brilliant in their smart uniforms, accompanied by the Regimental Band, march across to the Palace from the Wellington Barracks in Birdcage Walk for the changing of the Guard. The ceremony lasts half an hour and is very popular at the height of the tourist season, so if you want a good view it is best to get there early. For more details of winter times, ring the London Tourist Board: 01-730 0791.

*Tube:* Victoria, St James's Park.
*Bus:* 2, 2b, 9, 10, 11, 14, 16, 16a, 19, 22, 24, 25, 29, 30, 36, 36a, 38, 39, 52, 73, 74, 76, 137, 149, 185, 500, 503, 507.

## Royal Mews,
Buckingham Palace Road, SW1.

Around the corner from Buckingham Palace is the Royal Mews, where a heraldic lion and unicorn sit either side of the gateway. Look out for the colourful Coronation Coach and the exquisite royal horses. Open Wednesday and Thursday 2.00–4.00 pm.

Nearest tube and buses as above.

## Changing the Guard,
Horse Guards Parade, Whitehall, SW1.

Just across the park from the palace, in a small courtyard off Horse Guards Parade, yet another colourful spectacle takes place, when the Queen's Life Guard change the Guard, and then ride off down the Mall. This takes place daily at 11.00 am, and 10.00 am on Sunday. In the afternoon there is also a daily inspection of the Queen's Life Guard at 4.00 pm. Splendidly ceremonial, they sit on their beautifully groomed horses and carry out their duties with a stillness which is quite remarkable.

*Tube:* Charing Cross, Embankment.
*Bus:* 3, 11, 12, 24, 29, 53, 77, 77a, 77c, 88, 159, 168, 170, 172.

## Kensington Palace and Gardens,

The Broadwalk, Kensington Gardens, W8.
The cosiest palace in London and small enough not to tire even the
youngest child. Here you can see the rooms in which Queen
Victoria lived as a young princess, mementoes of her childhood,
her nursery, including her doll's house, toys, furniture, clothes,
jewellery and even the cradle she slept in. If all this proves too
much for young minds, opposite the palace across the Broad Walk
is the Round Pond. You are allowed to sail boats here and feed
ducks and geese. It is also an excellent place for kite spotting or
flying your own.

Further north, towards the Bayswater Road, is a large playground and just outside you will find the Elfin Oak with its carved
goblins, elves and fairies. In fact Kensington Gardens is a kind of
fairyland because Peter Pan also has his home there. His statue
stands on the west bank of the Long Water.

The Palace is open Monday to Saturday 10.00 am to 6.00 pm
and on Sunday from 2.00 until 6.00 pm. In winter the Palace closes
an hour earlier. Further information on the gardens can be found
on page 33.

*Tube:*   Queensway from the north side, High Street Kensington
          from the south side.
*Bus:*    9, 9a, 12, 27, 28, 31, 33, 49, 52, 73, 88.

## Commonwealth Institute,

Kensington High Street, W8. Tel: 01-602 3252.
Open Monday to Saturday 10.00 am–5.30 pm. Sunday: 2.30–5.00
pm.

Although this might not seem the most likely place for small
children to visit, there is a surprising amount to see and do here.
Each Commonwealth country has its own exhibition gallery, with a
number of interesting displays such as a space-age motorized
toboggan to ride on, called a "skidoo", in the Canadian section.
Also in the Institute are a variety of unusual stuffed birds and
animals, and in the New Zealand section a mechanical see-through
cow – just press a button and miraculously she will light up and
start making milk. In the Pacific Islands you can wander round
icebergs and penguins, meet a Royal Bengal tiger from Bangladesh
or say hello to a family of elephants in the Zambian section. If you

feel like a walk after your visit, Holland Park lies just behind the Institute. For more details see p. 37.

*Tube:* Kensington High Street.

*Bus:* 9, 27, 28, 31, 33, 49, 73.

**Big Ben,**

Parliament Square, SW1.

The King of Clocks and the most famous time-machine in the world. Big Ben is in fact the name of the great bell inside the tower, over a hundred years old, and the heaviest bell ever cast in Britain. He chimes once an hour and the four smaller bells round him chime the quarter and half hours.

*Tube:* Westminster.

*Bus:* 3, 11, 12, 24, 29, 53, 70, 76, 77, 77a, 77c, 88, 109, 155, 159, 168, 170, 172, 184, 503.

**Heathrow Airport,**

Middlesex. Tel: 01-759 4321.

A chance for plane-spotters to have a field day, and you can fly the tube direct to Heathrow on the Piccadilly line. Above the Queen's Building is the Spectators' Roof Garden where you can see all the different planes taking off and landing. Concorde arrives and departs every day and on Saturday morning you can see it leave at 9.00 and 11.15 am (check times before you go).

For light relief, if the noise of jet engines is too much, there is a small playground and café. The Roof Garden is open every day from 10.00 am until 5.00 pm.

*Tube:* Heathrow Central.

*Bus:* 82, 105, 140, 223, 285, 81, 222 to Heathrow North.

*Green Line:* 701, 704, 705, 724, 726, 727, 734.

## Zoos

**London Zoo,**

Regent's Park, NW1. Tel: 01-722 3333.

Open daily 9.00 am–6.00 pm. (November to March 10.00 am–6.00 pm.) Under-5s go in free. Admission is half price on the first Saturday of each month, except in June, July and August. Push-chairs can be hired and there is a lost child and first-aid room. There are facilities for nursing mothers too.

Situated in Regent's Park, just five minutes away from the West

End, London's famous zoo is one of the oldest and best known in the world. Over 9,000 animals live there but, tempting though it may be, don't feed them. In recent years new houses have been built for the monkeys, apes and big cats, giving them more space in natural surroundings. You can rub noses with the lions at the glass-fronted area of the lion terraces, or catch the elephants eating their daily snack of hay – they eat over two tons of it a week! During the summer months you can ride on the camels and donkeys, or take little excursions in llama or pony traps. To find out about new arrivals, babies or recent residents, check the notice board inside the main gate.

Especially for younger visitors, the Children's Zoo, set apart from the main zoo, gives an opportunity for those who spend their year in the city to meet some farm animals. From the three-foot-high green and brown spotted frog (actually a well camouflaged dustbin) to the large fluffy rabbits, all the animals you would expect are here. You can stroke the sheep, pigs and donkeys – but beware of the goats: it's true, they do eat anything. There is even a sign which warns, "The animals in this enclosure may try to eat your clothing, gloves and handbags, etc."

For hungry children there is a cafeteria on hand and also a playground with slides, tyre swings and climbing frames.

| Feeding Times: | Summer | Winter | |
|---|---|---|---|
| Sealions | 12 noon and 3.30 pm | 2.30 pm | not Fridays |
| Reptiles | 2.30 pm | 2.30 pm | Fridays only |
| Penguins | 2.30 pm | 2.30 pm | |
| Pelicans | 2.45 pm | 2.45 pm | |
| Birds of prey | 3.15 pm | 3.15 pm | not Thursdays. |

An interesting way of travelling to the zoo is to go on the Zoo Waterbus which runs a regular service from Little Venice and back. You buy an all-in ticket which includes the canal trip and entrance to the Zoo at a reduced price. During the summer months boats leave from 10.00 am (see page 24).

*Tube:*　Camden Town, Baker Street, Regent's Park.
*Bus:*　3, 53, 74.

## The London Butterfly House,

Syon Park, Brentford, Middx. Tel: 01-560 7272.
Open 10.00 am–5.00 pm daily.Under-5s go in free.

A unique opportunity to wander around tropical greenhouse gardens among free-flying butterflies from all over the world. All the various stages of development are in progress and in the insect exhibition adjoining the greenhouse you can see live giant spiders, leaf-cutting ants and scorpions.

*British Rail:* Kew Bridge via Waterloo, then 237 ot 267 bus to Brent Lea Gate.

*Tube:* Gunnersbury, then bus 237 or 267 to Brent Lea Gate.

## GLC Children's Zoos

There are GLC children's zoos in Battersea Park and Crystal Palace and their Mobile Zoo tours the Greater London parks during the summer months. No lions and tigers here but monkeys, rabbits, hamsters and a meerkat (a mixture between a large rat and a bushbaby). You pay a minimal charge for pony rides but the rest is free. For details of the Mobile Zoo's summer programme telephone 01-633 1691.

## Farms

The bricks and mortar of Greater London have spread out further and further in recent years. Yet in the middle of all this development the opportunities to see a slice of country life have increased. London is one of the few capitals in the world where a number of active small farms can be found within the city limits. Unlike many country farms, these little rural oases welcome visitors. While the London Zoo offers a close-up view of animals from all over the world, the city farms give children the chance to see feeding and milking time close to home. Depending on the farm you visit you can see all kinds of different animals ranging from goats and pigs to chickens, ponies and rabbits.

Ideal for 5s and under, the City farms listed below give them an opportunity to touch as well as look at a variety of animals, including chickens, rabbits, cows, goats and ponies.

## Express Dairy Farm,

River Lane, Petersham. Tel: 01-940 6211.
Off River Lane in Petersham Village is the Express Dairy Farm,

where at 3.00 pm you are able to see the cows being brought in to be milked. Milking itself starts at 3.45 pm and there are more than 32 cows to be seen as well as some calves. Each cow is known by name – Dolly, Moira, Lulu, Floss, Wilma, Folly and Jane are but a few.

*Tube:*   Richmond.

*Bus:*   65.

**Freightliners Farm,**

Paradise Park, Sheringham Road, N7. Tel: 01-609 0467.

Open 10.00 am–6.00 pm. Closed Monday.

*Tube:* Highbury & Islington, Caledonian Road.

*Bus:*   14, 43, 104, 271, 279.

**Inter-Action City Farm,**

1 Cressfield Close, off Grafton Road, NW5. Tel: 01-485 4585.

Open every day 10.00 am–5.00 pm.

*Tube:*   Kentish Town.

*Bus:*   24.

**Mudchute Community Farm,**

Pier Street, E14. Tel: 01-515 5901.

Open every day 9.00 am–5.00 pm. Closed lunchtime from 1.00–2.00 pm.

*Tube:*   Mile End.

*Bus:*   277.

**Spitalfields Community Farm,**

Buxton Street, E1. Tel: 01-247 8762.

Check opening times.

*Tube:*   Shoreditch.

**Stepney Stepping Stones Farm,**

Stepney Way, E1. Tel: 01-790 8204.

Open daily 9.30 am–6.00 pm, 9.30 am–8.00 pm at weekends.

*British Rail:*   Stepney East.

*Tube:*   Stepney Green.

*Bus:*   5, 10, 15, 23, 25, 40, 46.

**Surrey Docks Farm,**

Dog and Duck Passage, off Gulliver Street, SE16. Tel: 01-231 1010.

Open all week (except Monday) 10.00 am–5.00 pm.

*Tube:*   Surrey Docks, then bus P5.

**Vauxhall City Farm,**
24 St Oswald's Place (back entrance Tyers Street), SE11. Tel: 01-582 4204.
Open most days from 9.30 am until 5.30 pm, but check before you make your visit.
*Tube:* Vauxhall.
*Bus:* 2, 2b, 36, 36b, 44, 77, 88, 168a, 170, 185.

**City Farms Advisory Service,**
15 Wilkin Street, NW5. Tel: 01-403 0881.
Have a full list of farms, and produce a newsletter, *City Farm News.*

# PARKS, GARDENS AND PLAYGROUNDS

The Greater London Council looks after more than 5,000 acres of parkland and open spaces. Although these are some of the most likely places to visit when planning an outing, many of them have special recreational facilities that are often overlooked.

Opening times vary, depending on the season. For general information on Royal Parks, telephone Ministry of Public Buildings and Works, 01-735 7611; other parks, GLC Parks Office, 01-836 5464.

## Royal Parks

Originally all London's parkland was owned by the reigning monarch. Gradually whole areas were given to the people and to this day they are still known as the Royal Parks.

### Greenwich Park,

SE10. Tel: 01-858 2608.

Laid out specifically to order by a landscape gardener for King Charles II, it's worth making the steep climb to the top of the hill in Greenwich Park, where the view is one of the finest in London. Stand on the same hill with one foot either side of a simple brass strip and you will be on both sides of the world at the same time, for this is the site of the Old Royal Observatory and the brass strip is the line of zero longitude from which Greenwich Mean Time is calculated. Since the Observatory was first built in 1675 it has held a unique position in world astronomy.

*British Rail:*  Maze Hill.
*Tube:*  Surrey Docks, then bus 1a, 70, 108b, 188.
*Bus:*  53, 54, 75, 177, 180, 185.

### Hyde Park,

W1. Tel: 01-262 5484.

Over 630 acres of parkland – it seems a miracle that so much free space in the heart of London has remained untouched for so long. Good pushchair country as it is relatively flat, and if you walk to the Serpentine you will find boats to sail, birds to feed and on a summer day the Lido with its sandpit and paddling-pool.

*Tube:*  Hyde Park Corner, Knightsbridge, Lancaster Gate, Marble Arch.
*Bus:*  2, 2b, 9, 9a, 12, 14, 16, 16a, 19, 22, 25, 26, 30, 36, 36a, 38, 52, 73, 74, 74b, 88, 137, 500.

**Kensington Gardens,**

W2 and W8. Tel: 01-937 4848.

Adjoining Hyde Park is Kensington Gardens where the Serpentine becomes the Long Water. Parkland changes and among the trees and open spaces there are formal gardens, flower walks and fountains. Here, on the west bank of the Long Water, near where J.M. Barrie used to live, is the famous statue of Peter Pan, commemorating his well-known story. Immortalized in bronze and shined by countless hands, Peter Pan is joined by Wendy and surrounded by squirrels, mice and fairies. (For more details of the gardens see p. 26.)

*Tube:*  Lancaster Gate, Queensway, High Street Kensington.

*Bus:*  9, 12, 27, 28, 31, 33, 49, 52, 73, 88.

**Regent's Park,**

NW1. Tel: 01-486 7905.

This park was once a royal hunting ground, and although the deer have long since gone, there are now beautiful gardens to walk through, a playground and a lake teeming with birds. Here you can take out rowing boats, or if that sounds too energetic simply sit back and watch everyone else.

*Tube:*  Regent's Park, Baker Street, Camden Town, Great Portland. Street.

*Bus:*  1, 2, 2b, 3, 13, 18, 27, 30, 53, 74, 113, 137, 159, 176.

**Richmond Park,**

Richmond, Surrey. Tel: 01-948 3209.

The largest of London's parks, covering an area of ten square miles, Richmond Park was once the hunting ground of King Charles I; fortunately the deer have remained and still roam freely. It is important to explain to children that they must not feed or frighten the deer who although normally placid can be dangerous when approached too closely, especially in the mating season. In addition to the herds of red and fallow deer these many acres of woodland and open space make a perfect home for all manner of wild life. On Pen Ponds and the smaller ponds near the Richmond and Sheen Gates, you can feed the ducks and other water birds, or sail model boats.

About 500 yards from the Richmond Gate entrance is Penbroke Lodge. Here there is a restaurant with a self-service snackbar, open

every day from 1 January to 31 October, from 10.00 am until 30 minutes before the park closes. From 1 November until 31 December, it is open at weekends only, from 10.30 am until 30 minutes before closing time.
*Tube:* Richmond, then bus 65 or 71; Putney Bridge, then bus 85.
*British Rail:* Richmond.
*Bus:* 33, 37, 72, 73.

**St James's Park,**
SW1. Tel: 01-930 1793.
It is difficult to imagine that St James's Park was once a stretch of desolate marshland. Today it is one of the most glorious parks in London. From the rangy pink pelicans standing stiffly in their sanctuary by the lake to the tame ducks and wild fowl which you can feed yourself, it is rather like being in the garden of a rich stately home. An ideal park for small children as they can see the pelicans being fed in the afternoons at 4.00 pm and let off steam afterwards in the playground nearby.
*Tube:* St James's Park, Green Park.
*Bus:* 9, 14, 19, 22, 25, 38 to St James's Street.

## Other Parks
**Alexandra Park,**
N22. Tel: 01-444 7696.
Situated at the foot of Alexandra Palace overlooking Central London this extensive park has a children's play area, boating lakes, paddling-pool and Ski Centre (open October to April – tel: 01-888 2284). There is always something going on in the park during the holidays but check to find out more details of current events.
*Tube:* Finsbury Park, then bus W2, W3 or W7; or Wood Green, then bus W3.

**Archbishop's Park,**
Lambeth Road, SE1. Tel: 01-928 7592.
Ten acres of lawns and flowerbeds adjoining Lambeth Palace, plus a playground and children's shows in the summer.
*Tube:* Westminster, then walk across the bridge.
*Bus:* 3, 10, 44, 77, 149, 159, 168, 170, 507.

**Battersea Park,**
SW11. Tel: 01-228 2798.
Even though the funfair has gone there is still a boating lake,
paddling-pool, sandpit and a one o'clock club. In the summer
months, from April to September, the children's zoo is also open.
*Tube:*   Sloane Square, then bus 137; or South Kensington then
          bus 49.
*British Rail:*   Battersea Park.
*Bus:*    19, 39, 44, 170, 249, 295.

**Blackheath,**
SE3. Tel: 01-858 1692.
Once the haunt of highwaymen, this wide open space is now the
home of mobile zoos and travelling shows and fairs. It is also one of
the best places for a spot of kite flying.
*British Rail:*   Blackheath.
*Bus:*    53, 54, 75, 89, 108, 108b, 192.

**Broomfield Park,**
Broomfield Avenue, Palmers Green, N13. Tel: 01-886 8405.
One of North London's prettiest parks, and on those wetter days
there is the park museum to visit (see page 41).
*Tube:*   Wood Green.
*Bus:*    29, 123.

**Clissold Park,**
Green Lanes, N4. Tel: 01-800 1021.
There is an animal enclosure in the park with deer, peacocks,
cranes and a small aviary filled with tropical birds. The playground
has a paddling-pool.
*Tube:*   Manor House.
*Bus:*    106, 141, 171.

**Crystal Palace Park,**
SE19. Tel: 01-778 7148.
Twenty enormous plaster dinosaurs that once belonged to the
Great Exhibition of 1851 have taken over the islands in the middle
of the boating lake at Crystal Palace Park. For a glimpse of some
livelier animals, head straight for the children's zoo nearby. It's
open from April to September.
*Tube:*   Brixton, then buses 2b, 3.
*British Rail:*   Crystal Palace.
*Bus:*    12, 12a, 63, 108b, 122, 137, 154, 157, 227, 249.

**Dulwich Park,**
SE21. Tel: 01-693 5737.
Seventy-two acres of parkland with an aviary, boating lake, plus a full programme of children's entertainment in the summer.
*Tube:*   Brixton, then bus 3.
*Bus:*     12, 78, 176, 176a, 185.
**Finsbury Park,**
N4. Tel: 01-263 5001.
One of North London's smaller parks but nevertheless interesting for a day out, with its boating lake and summer travelling puppet shows.
*Tube:*   Finsbury Park.
*Bus:*     4, 19, 106, 230, 259, 279.
**Golders Hill Park,**
NW11. Tel: 01-455 5183.
An extension of Hampstead Heath, Golders Hill has a lake and a small zoo with deer, goats and a variety of different birds. For the adventurous, there are play sculptures, and for refreshment a convenient café. In summer the park is on the rounds of the touring children's theatres.
*Tube:*   Golders Green, then bus 210 or 268.
**Hampstead Heath,**
NW3. Tel: 01-485 4548.
Come well prepared – high on this famous heath there is a lot to do. Kite flying, sailing model boats, fishing, paddling or just walking and taking in the panoramic view of London below. On Bank Holidays there is always a fair, but whenever you go the Heath will provide numerous opportunities for enjoyment.
*Tube:*   Hampstead, Golders Green, then bus 210 or 268.
*Bus:*     24, 46, 187, 210, 268.
**Highgate Woods,**
N10.
An attractive area of woodland, made exciting to explore because of its hills and dips and the tiny squirrels that seem almost tame. There is a children's playground and paddling-pool.
*Tube:*   Highgate.
*Bus:*     43, 104, 134, 263.

### Holland Park,

W8. Tel: 01-602 2226.

A small park with well laid-out gardens to wander through, some woodland, squirrels and rabbits to see, peacocks and other exotic birds to feed. The café near the Orangery at Holland House is open from Easter to November, and there is an adventure playground for over-7s and a one o'clock club next door for under-5s.

*Tube:* Holland Park, Kensington High Street.
*Bus:* 9, 12, 27, 28, 31, 49, 73, 88.

### Ravenscourt Park,

Paddenswick Road, W6. Tel: 01-741 2051.

With its paddling-pool, sandpit, slides and climbing-frames, this park is ideal for small children. Thee is a one o'clock club and a small café nearby.

*Tube:* Ravenscourt Park.
*Bus:* 27, 88, 237, 266.

### Victoria Park,

E2. Tel: 01-985 1957.

The largest park in East London, laid out with gardens and a boating lake. There is a small compound with guinea-pigs, rabbits and chickens, and a separate enclosure which is the permanent home of a small herd of fallow deer. A good time to visit this park is in the early summer when you can see the baby deer. The GLC Mobile Zoo also comes here, usually for a week during August.

*Tube:* Bethnal Green; Mile End, then bus 277.
*Bus:* 8, 30, 106, 277.

### Syon Park,

Brentford, Middlesex. Tel: 01-560 0884.

Gardens and conservatory open daily 10.00 am–6.00 pm. Garden Centre 9.30 am–5.15 pm. On Sundays it opens and closes half an hour later. Check for winter opening times.

Acres of glorious parkland and gardens reaching down to the Thames, plus a conservatory that houses an aviary and aquarium. For those with green fingers there is the garden centre, one of the largest in the country.

*British Rail:* Kew Bridge via Waterloo. Cross the road for buses 237, 267 to Brent Lea Gate.
*Tube:* Gunnersbury, then 237, 267 bus to Brent Lea Gate; Hammersmith, then bus 267.

## Kew Gardens,

Kew, Surrey. Tel: 01-940 1171.

It will cost you 10 pence to enter Kew Gardens, and considering they are the most famous botanical gardens in the world it's a bargain. You can explore the tropical glass-houses, picnic near the Pagoda or simply walk along the scent-filled paths and make believe you are in the country. As the gardens cover nearly 300 acres it can be a problem deciding where to begin. For a first visit, enter by the main gates and a short walk will take you to Kew Palace. Originally called the Dutch House, this small red-brick building has an unexpectedly homely appearance for a once-royal residence. From the upstairs landing window you can see neatly laid-out gardens and the Thames meandering past in the background. Also in the palace are some unusual pieces of royal paraphernalia: silver filigree rattles which look far too elegant to have been chewed on even by royal teeth, and counters made of ivory.

Tucked away in the south-west corner of the gardens is Queen Charlotte's cottage. Named after George III's wife, it was originally used as a picnic lodge without, then, the busy roar of jet engines above.

Opening times: Kew Gardens are open daily, except Christmas and New Year's day, from 10.00 am until dusk. Kew Palace is open from April to September, Monday to Saturday, 11.00–5.30 pm. Sunday 2.00–5.30 pm. Queen Charlotte's Cottage is open on Saturday and Sunday (including Easter weekend) from April to September, 11.00 am–5.30 pm.

## Wimbledon Common,

SW19.

With its 1000 acres of woods and heath, Wimbledon Common is perfect for a country ramble and is full of different species of birds and animals including deer; there are also some lakes and a windmill that houses a small museum. Here you can see models and photographs and find out how a windmill works. The museum is open on Saturday and Sunday, 2.00–5.00 pm. There is a small entrance fee.

*Tube:*   Putney Bridge, then bus 39, 74, 85, 85a, 93; or
          Wimbledon, then bus 93.

*Bus:*    28, 72, 168.

## Parks Summer Entertainment

For details of entertainment in the Royal Parks, telephone 01-212 3434, and for current information on what's on in London's other parks read the Parks Diary. The Diary, available free from GLC Parks Information Service, 01-633 1707, gives full details of all events and entertainment from April to November.

# MUSEUMS

If the word museum conjures up a picture of a dusty, forbidding place full of old relics, you could be in for a surprise. During the last decade they have changed their image and now some of the most exciting developments in the world find their way into exhibitions at all the major museums, and London is particularly rich in museums. 5-year-olds and under will probably treat them as a glorified Hamleys – somewhere to wander through and have fun in, which is as good an introduction as any. They may not stand and contemplate each individual exhibit for any great length of time, but there will always be something to excite their curiosity or catch their attention.

## Bethnal Green Museum of Childhood,

Cambridge Heath Road, E2. Tel: 01-980 2415.
Open Monday to Saturday 10.00 am–6.00 pm, 2.30–6.00 pm Sunday (closed on Friday).

One of the best museums for children, it has a light airy atmosphere, is small enough to cover in one visit and contains one of the finest collections of dolls' houses in the country. Also housed in the museum are some splendid dolls, different kinds of puppets, optical toys which show visual tricks and illusions, model armies, miniature engines and a host of other toys. Of more interest to parents, perhaps, is the selection of period wedding dresses and furniture on the first floor. Occasionally on a Thursday afternoon the museum puts on a children's session called "Time to Play and Time to Talk", when under-5s can listen to stories, paint and play. Playgroups and nursery schools can make bookings for specially planned sessions if notice is given in advance to the Education Officer.

On Saturday the art room is open from 11.00 am–1.00 pm and from 2.00–4.00 pm and all visitors are welcome to use it. The children can play on their own, paint and even weave and there are two workshop leaders on hand to help anyone who needs it. Although there is no refreshment room at the museum the small park next door is ideal for a picnic.

*Tube:* Bethnal Green.
*British Rail:* Cambridge Heath.
*Bus:* 8, 8a, 106, 253.

**Broomfield Museum and Park,**
Broomfield Avenue, Palmers Green, N13. Tel: 01-882 1354.
Closed Mondays.
A small but interesting museum with a collection of stuffed animals and birds whose natural habitat is the area around the park. Upstairs is a replica of a Victorian nursery, full of original toys and games.
*Tube:* Bounds Green; Arnos Grove.
*British Rail:* Palmers Green and Southgate.
*Bus:* 29, 123.

**Gunnersbury Park Museum,**
Gunnersbury Park, Acton, W3. Tel: 01-992 1612.
Open Monday to Friday from 1.00–5.00 pm from April to September. Saturday and Sunday from 2.00–6.00 pm and in winter 2.00–4.00 pm.

This local history museum situated in spacious grounds contains a small collection of dolls, dolls' houses and dolls' clothes. It also has a transport collection including two carriages, a pony trap, tandem, tricycle, penny-farthing and a quaint little milk pram.
*Tube:* Acton Town.
*Bus:* E3.

**Kew Bridge Engines,**
Green Dragon Lane, off Kew Bridge Road, Brentford, Middx. Tel: 01-568 4757.
Open Saturday and Sunday 11.00 am–5.00 pm, but closes an hour earlier from October to April.

This small steam-engine museum is actually situated in a nineteenth-century water-pumping station in Kew Bridge Road and shows half a century of steam-engine development. The arrival of electric pumps made the steam-pumping engines redundant in 1944, and it is wonderfully soothing and reassuring to hear these great old water giants at work. Four have been restored by the museum and at different times during the day you can see them at work.
*British Rail:* Kew Bridge.
*Tube:* Gunnersbury.
*Bus:* 15, 65.

## London Transport Museum,

39 Wellington Street, Covent Garden, WC2. Tel: 01-379 6344.
Open 10.00 am–6.00 pm daily.

Part of the old flower market in Covent Garden has now been taken over by the museum and there is a wealth of London Transport on show. Gleaming trams, horse buses, trolley buses and even an old wooden milk van are displayed here, as well as the more modern tube trains and railway locomotives. It's unfortunate that children may only look and not climb onto some of the exhibits, but to remedy this you can take a trip on a vintage bus that runs from the museum.

*Tube:*   Covent Garden, Leicester Square.
*Bus:*    1, 6, 9, 11, 13, 15, 24, 29, 77, 77a, 77c, 170, 176.

## Museum of London,

London Wall, EC2. Tel: 01-600 3699.
Open Tuesday to Saturday 10.00 am–6.00 pm. Sunday 2.00–6.00 pm. Closed Monday. Pushchairs available. Coffee shop in basement.

The Museum of London opened in the Barbican in 1976 and it tells the story of London and life in London from earliest times until the present day. Each gallery depicts the various stages of development in London's history and reconstructs the different periods. You can see ancient armour, Tudor jewellery, Victorian shops and a penny-farthing bicycle. On the podium level is the "Great Fire Experience", a detailed model of London as it was in 1666 when the Great Fire swept through destroying most of the city. The authentic sound-effects and realistic atmosphere give a vivid impression of what it must have been like and because each show only lasts for five minutes, it goes down extremely well with under-5s. Starting at 10.00 am, the Great Fire Experience runs continuously throughout the day. Before you leave, visit the basement for a close look at the Lord Mayor's Coach. Over 200 years old, this splendidly ceremonial carriage encrusted with fine gold leaf is still used today. It's interesting to note that the simple method of surrounding the whole coach with a trough of water prevents the wood from warping.

*Tube:*   St Paul's, Barbican.
*Bus:*    4, 141, 279a, 502; or 8, 22, 25, 501 to St Paul's then a
          short walk.

**Natural History Museum,**
Cromwell Road, SW7. Tel: 01-589 6323.
Open daily 10.00 am–6.00 pm, except Sunday 2.30–6.00 pm.

Don't be put off by the size of this museum, housed in its blue and grey stone palace, and before you go in take a look at all the animals sculptured on the outside. As you enter, the Diplodocus is there to greet you. Vast and ancient, this massive dinosaur stands guard over the museum and, considering he has been dead for over 135 million years, he's doing quite well.

The first place to aim for is the Whale Hall where you can see the giant Blue Whale itself, suspended in mid-air and over 90 feet (26 metres) long. It's sad to think that over-hunting throughout the centuries has brought this fine creature close to extinction. Here at least you are given a glimpse of what the world's largest mammal looks like, for the chances of seeing one in its natural environment are very remote indeed. Also on display are smaller species of whales and various members of the dolphin family. The first floor is literally stuffed with all kinds of animals from different parts of the world. Bears, bats, bush-babies and bison are all on show as well as lions, tigers, panthers and monkeys. During the month of August and over the Easter holidays the Family Centre is open from Tuesdays to Saturdays. It's packed full of different things to look at and examine. There are telescopes to peer through, animal noises to listen to and different animal shapes to colour.

For more information visit the museum's Visitors Resources Centre on the ground floor.
*Tube:* South Kensington.
*Bus:* 14, 30, 49, 74.

**Pollock's Toy Museum,**
1 Scala Street, W1. Tel: 01-636 3452.
Open Monday to Saturday 10.00 am–5.00 pm. Closed Sunday.

Step back in time and wander through this tiny museum tucked away in the heart of London. It spans two houses joined together and the steeply winding staircase takes you to room after room, each with its own particular theme and crammed to the hilt with different toys, toy theatres, dolls and dolls' houses from all over the world. Sooty has his own corner and there are musical bears and Edward bears, some of which are nearly a century old. Downstairs is the museum shop with cut-out theatres, jigsaws and large glass jars full of marbles the size of golf balls. They also stock beautiful doll's house furniture and kitchen equipment.

*Tube:*   Goodge Street.
*Bus:*    14, 24, 29, 73, 176.

**The Science Museum,**
Exhibition Road, SW7. Tel: 01-589 3456.
Open daily 10.00 am–6.00 pm, but Sunday 2.30–6.00 pm.

Last but not least, one of the most exciting museums to visit in London. There is so much to see that it's best, especially with small children, to concentrate first on the lunar module and then the Children's Gallery and transport section. On the ground floor is a marvellous lifesize exhibit showing man's first landing on the moon. The lunar module looks somewhat like Superman's space capsule and it seems incredible that the astronauts travelled so far in such a frail-looking machine. Downstairs in the Children's Gallery, gadget fiends can have the time of their lives. There are knobs to twiddle and buttons to press, and intrepid aviators can even learn about flying by using a take-off and landing simulator. There are also burglar alarms to be tested, a model lift to operate and one of the first self-opening doors to run through. Meanwhile, older members of the family can keep their feet firmly on the ground by looking at an authentic Victorian kitchen, complete to the last detail. You might have difficulty in moving on from the gallery, but if the children can be lured away, the transport section on the ground floor is just as exciting with its collection of cars, engines and buses both old and new. There is a café on the top floor of the museum.

*Tube:*   South Kensington.
*Bus:*    14, 30, 45, 49, 74.

# 3

# A Taste of School

## CLUBS AND CLASSES

Less than two out of ten 3-year-olds in Britain have nursery education. Although we are trailing a long way behind other European countries in providing for the under-5s (in France eight out of ten 3-year-olds are at nursery school), there are a growing number of alternative facilities available, particularly in Greater London. These help to fill the gap especially in areas where nursery schools are scarce.

### Nursery Schools

Nursery schools are a vitally important introduction to education. It is surprising, therefore, that there are so few about. Obviously some boroughs are better off than others but remember to check well in advance of your child's third birthday and find out what schools are available in your area. If there is a waiting list, the earlier your child's name goes on it the better.

Nursery schools are run by the local education authority and come under the Department of Education. They use trained teachers whose aim is to encourage the children to make use of a wide variety of different activities in a positive way and in a stimulating environment. The lessons are very informal and classes are initially for a half day, morning or afternoon. In the child's last year this is sometimes extended to a full day in preparation for primary school.

## Playgroups

Playgroups also cater for 3- to 5-year-olds although some do take children slightly younger. They are unique in so far as they work very much on the combined efforts of the playleaders, their assistants and voluntary help from parents themselves. Sessions are usually two and a half hours long and are held during term time, Monday to Friday. The equipment provided by most playgroups consists of a slide, climbing-frame, sand and water, paints, books, bricks and an assortment of toys and games. These will of course vary to a large extent on the funds available. Although parents are encouraged to play their part by regular attendance and help, at the same time they know they can leave their children in the care of the playgroup leaders. To find out where your nearest playgroup is, contact the Pre-School Playgroup Association (PPA), 314/316 Vauxhall Bridge Road, SW1. Tel: 01-828 1401 (Inner London); 01-828 2417 (Greater London).

### Courses for Playgroups

Playgroup leaders and assistants have all attended a course, or had some form of suitable training. These courses are run by ILEA in co-operation with the London PPA, and are open to anyone who is interested in working with young children. The foundation course runs for one day a week from 10.00 am until 3.00 pm for three terms and includes practical work and visits to nursery classes and playgroups. A certificate is given on completion. For further information contact the Inner London Pre-School Playgroup Association, 314/316 Vauxhall Bridge Road, SW1. Tel: 01-828 1401.

## One O'Clock Clubs

One o'clock clubs are usually based in public parks and are open all the year round. They start at one o'clock, as the name suggests, and finish at 4.00 pm from Monday to Friday. Some are run by the GLC while others are under the auspices of the local borough council and they enable children to get out and about with their parents and enjoy the activities provided by the club. One o'clock clubs are free and are run by experienced staff, but while children are there they must be accompanied by an adult. There is a club building which provides play materials and the play area outside is usually equipped with slides, a sandpit and climbing frames etc. To find out where your local one o'clock club is, contact the information office at your local town hall. Alternatively the GLC One O'Clock Club offices are at 285 Albany Road, SE5. Tel: 01-701 2046.

## Mother and Toddler Clubs

Unlike the one o'clock clubs which are generally run by borough councils or the GLC, mother and toddler clubs are organized in a variety of ways and each one offers different activities. One might be affiliated to a church hall or centre, while others have been successfully started and run by the mothers themselves. Their main value lies in providing an opportunity for children (and parents) to socialize together at an early stage. To find out more about mother and toddler clubs, contact the Pre-School Playgroup Association, 314/316 Vauxhall Bridge Road, SW1. Tel: 01-828 2417.

## Childminders

Some people are lucky enough to have neighbours who will look after their children when they need to go out. If there is no one close by whom you know and trust, your local social services department keep details and a current list of childminders who are registered with the council. They look after children in their own homes and are allowed to care for three under-5s, and that includes any children of their own. Once the initial introduction has been made, arrangements as to pay, hours, holidays etc. are settled by the parents and childminder.

## Music, Movement and Dance

Whatever their age, children take great delight in playing and listening to music. Movement and dance are a valuable and natural way of helping to improve co-ordination, whether through simple songs and nursery rhymes played at home or by taking it a step

further and joining one of the many classes available in the Greater
London area. Telephone to check availability and times.

**Battersea Arts Centre,**

Old Town Hall, Lavender Hill, SW11. Tel: 01-223 8413.

In addition to the activities covered earlier (p. 18) the Centre also
runs a beginners' ballet class on Saturday morning at 10.30 am for
3-year-olds and upwards. There are extra classes during the
holidays.

*British Rail:* Clapham Junction.

*Bus:*    77, 186.

**Chiswick Music Centre,**

Hounslow Borough College, Bath Road, Chiswick, W4. Tel:
01-994 3454.

During term time, classes are held on Mondays, Tuesdays and
Wednesdays, when 2- to 5-year-olds can learn how to play
percussion instruments, listen and move to music and sing songs.
Phone the college for details of times. Enrolment is for a minimum
of six weeks.

*Tube:*   Turnham Green.

*Bus:*    E3, 88.

**The Early Music Centre,**

137 Gosswell Road, EC1. Tel: 01-251 2304.

For 4- to 5-year-olds there is a simple introductory course to music
and dance of the Middle Ages and Renaissance period – Romeo and
Juliet style. This isn't as serious as it sounds and the classes involve
singing, movement and dance. Enrolment is for a term.

*Tube:*   Barbican, Angel.

*Bus:*    4, 5, 55, 243, 277.

**Eurhythmy,**

Rudolph Steiner House, 35 Park Road, NW1. Tel: 01-723 4400.

Don't be put off by the name; eurhythmy is the art of interpreting
speech and music through movement. Sounds and words can lend
themselves to a particular movement or shape and, through this,
language becomes visible. Small children begin by playing simple
ring games (Ring-a-ring-a-roses) or singing, clapping and jumping
to a well-known tune. By using their imagination in this way,
concentration improves and a different approach to music and

movement is achieved. Sessions for 3- to 5-year-olds are held on Saturday mornings. Classes are mixed and take place during term time only.
*Tube:* Baker Street.
*Bus:* 2, 2b, 13, 74, 113.
**Pineapple Dance Centre,**
7 Langley Street, Covent Garden, WC2. Tel: 01-836 4004.
Saturday lunchtime sessions take place here for 5-year-olds upwards at which they can tap their toes to the sound of pop music and learn a modern-dance routine.
*Tube:* Covent Garden, Leicester Square.
*Bus:* 1, 6, 9, 11, 13, 15, 24, 29, 77, 77a, 77c, 170, 176.

## Other Classes
**The Antonia Dugdale School of Dancing,**
7 Hamilton Terrace, NW8. Tel: 01-286 1741.
Dancing classes are held here and in Islington for children of 3 years old upwards on Monday, Tuesday, Wednesday and Thursday afternoons from 3.30 pm onwards. Pupils are expected to enrol for a term.
**Islington Dance Factory,**
Vergers Cottage, 2 Parkhurst Road, N7. Tel: 01-607 0561.
Classes for 4-year-olds and upwards take place on Wednesday and Friday afternoons.
**Daphne Miles School of Dancing,**
Wansted House Community Centre, 21 The Green, Wanstead, E11. Tel: 01-539 3376.
Classes for beginners, 4-year-olds and upwards, are on Thursday afternoons at 4.30 pm.
**Stella Mann School,**
343a Finchley Road, NW3. (Entrance in Lymington Road.) Tel: 01-435 9317.
Classes for 4-year-olds and upwards are on Tuesdays at 4.00 pm.
**Lilian Harmel Studio,**
37 Ferncroft Avenue, NW3.
Children are graded according to age and experience. For 4-year-olds classes are held on Saturday mornings, and in addition there are also classical ballet classes. For details write direct.

**Biddy Pinchard,**
The Studio, 20 Raleigh Gardens, Brixton Hill, SW2. Tel: 01-674
2348.
The studio is one of the few places to hold sessions for children as
young as 2½ years old. Their baby and beginners classes are on
Wednesdays at 4.00 pm and Saturday afternoons at 3.15 pm.
**Ballet Rambert School,**
Mercury Theatre, 2 Ladbroke Road, W11. Tel: 01-727 7233.
One of London's most famous dance companies, who also run
classes for children from the age of 4. Lessons are given every day
at 4.15 pm, and on Saturday mornings at 9.30, 10.30 and 11.30
am. Pupils enrol for a full term which runs for twelve weeks.
**Royal Academy of Dancing,**
Vicarage Crescent, SW11. Tel: 01-223 0091.
Classes for 5-year-olds are held on Saturday mornings. Enrolment
is for a term.
**The Saturday Music Centre at Acland Burghley School,**
Burghley Road, NW5. Tel: 01-485 8515.
Music and movement group on Saturday mornings during term
time for 3- to 5-year-olds.
**Oval House,**
54 Kensington Oval, SE11. Tel: 01-582 7680.
The beginners' dance technique workshop for 4- to 7-year-olds takes
place on Tuesday afternoons, 4.00–5.30 pm. Term time only.
**Urdang Academy,**
20–22 Shelton Street, WC1. Tel: 01-836 5709.
Saturday classes begin at 2.00 pm for 3-year-olds upwards.

# SPORT AND EXERCISE

More and more sports and leisure centres that are opening in London have facilities and hold sessions for 5-year-olds and under. Some, though unfortunately by no means all, also have crèches where parents using the centres can leave their children in safe hands. Check details in advance. Times vary from term to term.

**Britannia Leisure Centre,**
40 Hyde Road, N1. Tel: 01-729 4485.
Every morning during the holidays there are Baby Bounce sessions, where under-5s can climb, bounce and leap about on mini gymnastics equipment. During term-time, sessions are on Monday and Saturday only, 10.00–12.00 am.
*British Rail:* Dalston Junction.
*Tube:* Old Street.
*Bus:* 22, 22a, 30, 38, 48, 67, 73, 76, 141, 243a, 271.

**Bullsmoor Sports Centre,**
Bullsmoor Lane, Enfield, Middlesex. Tel: 01-971 8408.
The borough council have set up gymnastics classes at the Bullsmoor Centre as part of a gymnastics development plan. There are four different venues for these courses in the borough; for more information telephone the Civic Centre on 01-366 6565, extension 2345.
*British Rail:* Turkey Street, Waltham Cross.
*Bus:* Red 217, 217b. Green Line 734, 735.

**Crofton Leisure Centre,**
Manwood Road, Brockley, SE4. Tel: 01-690 0273.
Gymnastics for 5-year-olds (sometimes children are accepted into the class slightly younger) on Mondays at 5.15 pm (girls), Tuesdays at 5.00 pm (boys) and on Fridays there is a mixed class at 5.00 pm. For more information telephone 01-699 8856. There is also ballet for beginners (3- to 4-year-olds) on Thursdays and tap dancing for beginners on Mondays.
*British Rail:* Crofton Park, Catford, Catford Bridge.
*Bus:* 75, 108b, 141, 185.

**Eternit Wharf Recreation Centre,**
Stevenage Road, Fulham, SW6. Tel: 01-381 5266.
Judo and gymnastics classes held here, but there is a waiting list.

For 5-year-olds and under "roly-poly" mini-gymnastics session takes place on Thursdays at 2.30 pm.
*Tube:*   Hammersmith, Putney Bridge.
*Bus:*    11, 30, 74, 220.

**Ferndale Sports Centre,**
Nursery Road, SW9. Tel: 01-733 5703.
Gymnastics classes for 4-year-olds upwards on Tuesday afternoons. Extra activities are put on during the summer holidays.
*Tube:*   Brixton.
*Bus:*    2, 2b, 3, 5, 45, 95, 109, 133, 137, 159.

**Finsbury Leisure Centre,**
Norman Street, EC1. Tel: 01-253 2346.
Under-5 gymnastics take place on Wednesdays between 2.00 and 4.00 pm.
*Tube:*   Old Street.
*Bus:*    5, 55, 76, 141, 243, 271.

**Flaxman Sports Centre,**
Carew Street, SE5. Tel: 01-737 3273.
Trampolining and gymnastic sessions for 5-year-olds and under on Thursdays and Saturdays.
*Tube:*   Brixton.
*Bus:*    2b, 3, 35, 45, 50, 95, 109, 133, 159, 172.

**Harrow Leisure Centre,**
Christchurch Avenue, Harrow. Tel: 01-863 5611.
Pre-school gymnastics on Monday, Tuesday and Thursday afternoons.
*British Rail:*   Harrow and Wealdstone.
*Bus:*    H1 bus goes down Christchurch Avenue; 114, 182, 186, 258, 286 go to the station.

**Lewisham Leisure Centre,**
Rennell Street, SE13. Tel: 01-318 4421.
Under-5s gymnastic sessions on Mondays, Wednesdays and Thursdays from 10.00 am.
*British Rail:* Lewisham.
*Bus:*    1, 21, 36, 47, 70, 94, 180, 185.

**Pickett's Lock Leisure Centre,**
Pickett's Lock Lane, N9. Tel: 01-803 4756.
There are Baby Bounce sessions on Tuesday and Thursday after-

noons from 2.00 to 4.00 pm, where under-5s can stretch their limbs and bounce on the mini trampolines.
*British Rail:*  Lower Edmonton.
*Bus:*  W8.
### Rugby Club,
223 Walmer Road, W11. Tel: 01-229 7097.
Providing they can manage a simple forward roll, 4- to 5-year-olds can join the beginners' gymnastic classes on Tuesdays and Thursdays at 4.30 pm. Term time only.
*Tube:*  Ladbroke Grove, Latimer Road.
*Bus:*  7, 15, 52.
### Michael Sobell Sports Centre,
Hornsey Road, N7. Tel: 01-607 1632.
The under-5s play session takes place from Monday to Friday, 1.00–4.00 pm. All parents who have children between the ages of 2 and 5 are welcome, but you must supervise your children throughout the session. The Sobell also runs hourly sessions, when they can use the mini gymnastic equipment. Sessions can be booked through reception 7 days in advance. There is also a Ladies' Programme on Tuesdays and Thursdays from 1.00 to 4.00 pm, with a keep-fit class, squash, badminton and a crèche for children aged between 2 and 5. (For more details of crèches see page 86.)
*Tube:*  Finsbury Park, Holloway Road.
*Bus:*  4, 14, 17, 19, 29, 43, 104, 168a, 172, 221, 259, 263, 279, 279a.
### Vale Farm Sports Centre,
Watford Road, Wembley, Middx. Tel: 01-908 2528.
For 3- to 5-year-olds there is a keep-fit class on Tuesday afternoons at 4.30 pm.
*Tube:*  Sudbury Town.
*Bus:*  182.
### Wanstead Sports Centre,
Redbridge Lane West, off Eastern Avenue, E11. Tel: 01-989 1172.
Judo and trampoline courses are run here for 5-year-olds and over.
*Tube:*  Redbridge, Wanstead.
*Bus:*  66, 101, 148, 162, 206.

**Jubilee Hall Recreational Centre,**
Central Market Square, Covent Garden, WC2. Tel: 01-836 4835.
Acrobatic sessions are held at the Centre on Saturday mornings.
Nimble 4- and 5-year-olds should go along at 10.00 am.
*Tube:*   Covent Garden, Leicester Square.
*Bus:*      1, 6, 9, 11, 13, 15, 24, 29, 77, 77a, 77c, 170, 176.

# Swimming

For most children playing in the bath is as natural as washing is
distasteful. In order not to lose this enjoyment an introduction to a
swimming-pool as early as possible is the best way of preserving
their interest in water and eliminating any possible fear. Listed
below are swimming baths that have small "learner" pools. In most
cases special times are set aside when parents with small children
can use the pool. This is an excellent opportunity for children to
play together, learn to swim and feel confident because you are
there. At some pools swimming instruction is available. For details
of lessons and opening times, check with your local baths.

**Camden Baths,**
Grafton Road, Kentish Town, NW5. Tel: 01-485 3678.
**Chelsea Baths,**
Chelsea Manor Street, SW3. Tel: 01-352 6985.
**Clapham Baths,**
Clapham Manor Street, SW4. Tel: 01-622 2786.
**Copthall Pool,**
Page Street, NW7. Tel: 01-203 4187.
**Crystal Palace Sports Centre,**
Ledrington Road, SE19. Tel: 01-778 0131.
**Elephant and Castle Leisure Centre,**
Elephant and Castle, SE1. Tel: 01-582 5505.
**Essex Road Baths,**
Greenman Street, off Essex Road, N1. Tel: 01-226 3655.
**Ironmonger Row Baths,**
Ironmonger Row, EC1. Tel: 01-253 4011.
**Kensington Baths,**
Walmer Road, W11. Tel: 01-727 9418.

**Lewisham Baths,**
Ladywell, Lewisham High Street, SE13. Tel: 01-690 2123.
**Leytonstone Recreation Centre,**
Cathall Road, Leytonstone, E11. Tel: 01-539 8343.
**Park Road Baths,**
Park Road, N8. Tel: 01-348 9484.
**Pickett's Lock Leisure Centre,**
Pickett's Lock Lane, Edmonton, N9. Tel: 01-803 4756.
**Putney Baths,**
Upper Richmond Road, SW15. Tel: 01-789 1124.
**Queen Mother Sports Centre,**
Vauxhall Bridge Road, SW1. Tel: 01-834 4725.
**Swiss Cottage Baths,**
Winchester Road, NW3. Tel: 01-278 4444.
**White City Pool,**
Bloemfontein Road, White City, W12. Tel: 01-743 3401.

In some areas such as Elephant and Castle or White City, the so-called "leisure pool" has taken over from the conventional oblong one. These have a gentle shelving bottom just like a beach, and to complete the picture and to increase the play element there are tropical plants and a wave machine. Surely an ideal way of swimming without tears!

## Ice Skating
Children have been known to start ice skating from the age of 2; the problem is getting skates small enough. Rinks only hire them out from size seven, so, if after visiting an ice pantomime your little one feels like heading for the nearest rink, telephone first to make sure they have the right skates for hire.

**Queen's Ice Skating Club,**
Queensway, W2. Tel: 01-229 0172.
**Richmond Ice Rink,**
Clevedon Road, Twickenham. Tel: 01-892 3646.
**Sobell Sports Centre,**
Hornsey Road, N7. Tel: 01-607 1632.
**Streatham Ice Rink,**
386 Streatham High Road, SW16. Tel: 01-769 7861.

## Roller Skating

Roller skating is now more popular than ever and quite a number of roller rinks in the London area have sessions for children. Always telephone before you go to check times and to find out if they have the right size skates for hire

**Alexandra Palace,**
Wood Green, N22. Tel: 01-444 7203.
**Electric Ballroom,**
184 Camden High Street, NW1. Tel: 01-485 9006.
**Finsbury Leisure Centre,**
Norman Street, EC1. Tel: 01-253 4490.
**Harrow Leisure Centre,**
Christchurch Avenue, Harrow, Middx. Tel: 01-863 9580.
**Jubilee Hall Recreation Centre,**
Central Market Square, Covent Garden, WC2. Tel: 01-836 2799.
**Pickett's Lock Leisure Centre,**
Pickett's Lock Lane, Edmonton, N9. Tel: 01-803 4756.
**Starlight Roller Disco,**
208 Shepherd's Bush Road, W6. Tel: 01-603 2901.
**Tottenham Sports Centre,**
703 High Road, N17. Tel: 01-801 6401.

# BOOKS AND TOYS

## Children's Libraries

Junior libraries cater for children of all ages including stories and picture books for 5s and under. No one is too young to join, and miniature tables and chairs make it easier for small children to sit and enjoy the different books. Three books can normally be borrowed for up to a period of three weeks and no fines are charged, although you will be sent reminder notices if books become overdue. Children's libraries can also be helpful in other ways. They have useful "what's on" information and often have special children's activities during the holidays. Some children's libraries have a mobile bus for those who can't get out, and a few main libraries have a record and tape selection that you can borrow. Phone the Library Association, 01-636 7543, for information about facilities for children in libraries. To find out where your nearest Junior Library is, contact:

| | |
|---|---|
| Balham | – 01-673 4119 |
| Barnet | – 01-349 9121 ext. 366 |
| Battersea | – 01-228 3474 |
| Camden | – 01-278 4444 ext. 3019 |
| City of Westminster | – 01-828 8070 ext.4041 |
| Ealing | – 01-574 7029 |
| Greenwich | – 01-858 6656 ext. 35 |
| Hackney | – 01-985 8262 |
| Hammersmith | – 01-748 6032 |
| Islington | – 01-609 3051 |
| Kensington and Chelsea | – 01-937 2542 |
| Lambeth | – 01-274 7451 |
| Lewisham | – 01-698 7347 |
| Richmond | – 01-940 0031 |
| Southwark | – 01-693 9221 |
| Tower Hamlets | – 01-980 4366 |
| Wandsworth | – 01-874 1143 |

Listed below is a selection of favourite under-5s reading. Other suggestions can be found in *Reading for Enjoyment with 0–6 year-*

*olds* by Dorothy Butler (Baker Book Services), *Spare Rib List of Non-Sexist Children's Books* compiled by Rosemary Stones and Andrew Mann, *Penguin Multi-Ethnic Book List* (free) by Rosemary Stones, and *Non-Sexist Picture Books,* a list compiled by the women's group CISSY (Campaign to Impede Sex Stereotyping in the Young, 177 Gleneldon Road, SW16); the thrice-yearly *Children's Book Bulletin* (4 Aldebert Terrace, SW8 – enclose s.a.e. for further information) provides news about "progressive moves in children's literature". Don't forget that most libraries also have lists of books recommended for young children. The Children's Reference Library (c/o National Book League, 45 East Hill, SW18. Tel: 01-870 9055) keeps a copy and records of most recently published children's books.

Janet and Allan Ahlberg: *Each Peach, Pear and Plum* (Kestrel)
Brian Alderson: *Cakes and Custard* (Heinemann)
Edward Ardizzone: *Diana and her Rhinoceros* (Bodley Head)
Edward Ardizzone: *Tim* books (Oxford University Press)
Edward Ardizzone: *Paul, the Hero of the Fire* (Kestrel)
Alan Arkin and James Stevenson: *Tony's Hard Work Day* (Deutsch/ Collins Picture Lions)
Nicola Bayley: *Book of Nursery Rhymes* (Cape)
Val Biro: *Gumdrop* series (Hodder and Stoughton/Piccolo)
Petronella Breinburg: *Sally-Ann* and *Sean* books (Bodley Head)
Raymond Briggs: *The Mother Goose Treasury* (Hamish Hamilton)
Jean de Brunhoff: *The Story of Babar* (Methuen)
John Burningham: *ABC* (Cape)
John Burningham: *Mr Gumpy's Motor Car* (Cape/Puffin)
John Burningham: *Mr Gumpy's Outing* (Cape/Puffin)
Eric Carle: *The Bad-Tempered Ladybird* (Hamish Hamilton)
Eric Carle: *The Very Hungry Caterpillar* (Cape)
Ruth Craft: *The Winter Bear* (Collins Picture Lions)
Graham Greene: *The Little Train* (Bodley Head/Puffin)
Russell Hoban: *A Bargain for Frances* (World's Work)
Russell Hoban: *Bedtime for Frances* (Faber/Puffin)
Russell Hoban: *Best Friends for Frances* (Faber/Puffin)
Shirley Hughes: *Alfie Gets in First* (Gollancz)
Shirley Hughes: *Lucy and Tom at the Seaside* (Gollancz/Carousel)

Shirley Hughes: *Lucy and Tom Go to School* (Gollancz/Carousel)
Shirley Hughes: *Lucy and Tom's Day* (Gollancz)
Pat Hutchins: *Don't Forget the Bacon* (Bodley Head/Puffin)
Pat Hutchins: *Happy Birthday, Sam* (Puffin)
Pat Hutchins: *Rose's Walk* (Bodley Head/Puffin)
Pat Hutchins: *Titch* (Bodley Head/Puffin)
Charles Keeping: *Shaun and the Carthorse* (Oxford University Press)
Judith Kerr: *Mog's Christmas* (Collins)
Judith Kerr: *Mog the Forgetful Cat* (Collins Picture Lions)
Judith Kerr: *The Tiger Who Came to Tea* (Collins Picture Lions)
Edward Lear: *The Quangle Wangle's Hat* (Puffin)
Helen Nicholl and Jan Pienkowski: *Meg and Mog* series (Heinemann/Puffin)
Ruth Orbach: *Acorns and Stew* (Collins Picture Lions)
Ruth Orbach: *One Eighth of a Muffin* (Collins Picture Lions)
Helen Oxenbury: *An ABC of Things* (Heinemann)
Oliver Postgate and Peter Firmin: *Ivor the Engine* books (Collins Picture Lions)
Alice and Martin Provensen: *The Year at Maple Farm* (Cape)
Mary Rayner: *Garth Pig and the Ice-cream Van* (Macmillan)
Mary Rayner: *Mr and Mrs Pig's Evening Out* (Macmillan/Puffin)
Diana Ross: *The Story of the Little Red Engine* (Faber/Puffin)
John Ryan: *Captain Pugwash* books (Bodley Head/Puffin)
Richard Scarry: *Animal Nursery Tales* (Collins Picture Lions)
Richard Scarry: *The Great Steamboat Mystery* (Collins Picture Lions)
Maurice Sendak: *Where the Wild Things Are* (Bodley Head/Puffin)
Shigeo Watanabe: *How Do I Put It On?* and other books (Bodley Head)
Gunilla Wolde: *Thomas and His Cat,* and other *Thomas and Emma* books (Hodder and Stoughton)
Kit Wright: *Arthur's Grannie* (Methuen)
Kit Wright: *Arthur's Uncle* (Methuen)
Thomas and Wanda Zacharias: *But Where is the Green Parrot?* (Chatto/Piccolo)

# Book Shops

**Bookboat,**
Cutty Sark Gardens, Greenwich, SE10. Tel: 01-853 4383.
London's only floating bookshop.

**Bookspread,**
58 Tooting Bec Road, SW17. Tel: 01-767 6377.

**Centrepiece,**
136–8 Kingsland High Street, E8. Tel: 01-254 9632.
Community bookshop.

**Children's Bookshop,**
29 Fortis Green Road, N10. Tel: 01-444 5500.

**Children's World,**
229 Kensington High Street, W8. Tel: 01-937 6314.
Largest children's bookshop in Europe.

**Claude Gill,**
24 Oxford Street, W1. No telephone number.

**Collets International Bookshop,**
129–31 Charing Cross Road, WC2. Tel: 01-734 0782.

**Foyles,**
119 Charing Cross Road, WC2. Tel: 01-437 5660.

**Harrods,**
Knightsbridge, SW1. Tel: 01-730 1234.

**Hatchards,**
187 Piccadilly, W1. Tel: 01-439 9921.

**High Hill Bookshop,**
6 Hampstead High Street, NW3. Tel: 01-435 2218.

**Lion and Unicorn Bookshop,**
19 King Street, Richmond. Tel: 01-940 0483.

**Pan Bookshop,**
158 Fulham Road, SW10. Tel: 01-373 4997.

**Reading Matters,**
22 Lymington Avenue, N22. Tel: 01-881 3187.
Community bookshop.

**John Sandoe,**
10 Blacklands Terrace, SW3. Tel: 01-589 9473.
A good selection of old favourites.

**Sisterwrite,**
190 Upper Street, N1. Tel: 01-226 9782.
Non-sexist children's books a speciality.

**Truslove and Hanson,**
205 Sloane Street, SW1. Tel: 01-235 2128.

There are a few shops specializing in Black and Third World books which have useful children's sections:
**New Beacon Books,**
76 Stroud Green Road, N4. Tel: 01-272 4889.
**Walter Rodney Bookshop,**
5a Chignell Place, West Ealing, W13. Tel: 01-579 4920.
**Sabarr Books,**
378 Coldharbour Lane, SW9. Tel: 01-274 6785.
**Soma Books,**
38 Kennington Lane, SE11. Tel: 01-735 2101.

## Book Events
**National Book League,**
The Book House, 45 East Hill, SW18. Tel: 01-870 9055.
An exhibition of children's books takes place at the National Book League every summer, usually some time in July.
**Publishers Assocation,**
19 Bedford Square, WC1. Tel: 01-580 6321.
The Publisher's Assocation organizes a National Children's Week, when special events are held all over the country.
**The Puffin Exhibition**
is held annually for ten days, usually at Easter. It gives you the opportunity to have a look at all the Puffin Books that have been printed for children and there is always a special section for 5s and under. To find out more, telephone The Puffin Club, 01-759 5722.

## Toy Libraries
Just as libraries lend books, toy libraries lend toys and provide an invaluable service for playgroups, play centres, foster parents and childminders. Initially they provided toys for handicapped children, but today they give every child with special needs the opportunity to experiment with a wide variety of toys. Recently a growing number of toy libraries have branched out and opened their doors to all children, and although they vary there is usually a nominal fee for membership. The lending arrangements are that you borrow one toy per child for a week or fortnight, and there

may be a small charge of 5p or 10p for the loan of each toy. Many
toy libraries are organized by voluntary groups, others are in
community centres, special hospitals, schools and clinics, and some
are within public book libraries. Listed below is a selection of
addresses for toy libraries within the London area (there would
probably be over a hundred on a full list). The Toy Libraries
Association is the parent body for toy libraries, offering advice and
support on all aspects of running a library and toy maintenance. It
provides comprehensive information on setting up a toy library and
encourages close liaison between toy libraries and the toy industry,
to increase the general availability of good toys.

To find out where your nearest toy library is, contact Lesley
Moreland, the Toy Libraries Association, Wyllyotts Manor, Darkes
Lane, Potters Bar, Herts. Tel: 0707 44571.

They also produce an indispensable book entitled *The Good Toy
Guide,* the only comprehensive guide of its kind in Britain. All the
900 widely available toys listed have been tested by the Toy
Libraries Assocation. Their panel of child specialists assessed each
toy on its play value, safety, durability in an effort to give parents
the best choice possible. The book can be ordered from a number
of bookshops or can be acquired direct from the Toy Libraries
Association.

E1    – Spitalfield Toy Libraries, c/o Montefiore Centre, Deal
          Street.
E8    – Children's Librarian, Dalston Library, 24 Dalston Lane.
E16   – Newham Play Association, 141 Newham Way, Canning
          Town.
E17   – Whitefield Toy Library, Whitefield School, Warner Road.
N1    – Upper Street Toy Library, c/o 90–92 Upper Street,
          Islington.
N19   – Caxton House Toy Library, 129 St John's Way, Upper
          Holloway.
N22   – Community Play Centre, 35 Station Road, Wood Green.
NW2   – Minster Day Nursery, 68 Shoot-Up Hill, Cricklewood.
NW6   – Carlton Nursery Centre, Granville Road, Kilburn.
SE1   – Toy Library, Newcomen Centre, Guy's Hospital, St
          Thomas Street.

SE11  – Childminders Toy Library, Hurley House, Kempsford Road.
SW2   – Brixton Child Guidance Unit, 19 Brixton Water Lane.
SW3   – Kensington & Chelsea Venture Toy Library, c/o Chelsea Playground, The Rectory Garden, 56 Old Church Street.
SW4   – Clapham Toy Library, St Ann's Hall, Venn Street.
SW5   – Under-5s Centre, 46 Longridge Road, Earls Court.
SW9   – Sheldon Toy Library, Belgrave Children's Hospital, Clapham Road.
W6    – Child Development Centre, Charing Cross Hospital (Fulham), Fulham Palace Road.
W10   – Toy Library, Kensal Health Centre, 4 Maxilla Walk.
W12   – Invalid Children's Aid Association, 3 Keith Grove.
WC1   – Toy Library, Department of Psychological Medicine, Hospital for Sick Children, Great Ormond Street.
WC1   – Toy Library Organiser, Thomas Coram Foundation for Children, 40 Brunswick Square.

## Toyshops

Here are some of the best toyshops that I have come across.

**Animus,**
84 Highgate Street, N6. Tel: 01-348 7381.
**Bagatelle Toys,**
79 High Street, SW19. Tel: 01-946 7981.
**Chatterbox,**
23 Church Street, Twickenham, Middx. Tel: 01-892 2481.
Unique in so far as they have a jigsaw library! A thirty-piece puzzle can be borrowed for up to a fortnight.
**Children's World,**
229 Kensington High Street, W8. Tel: 01-937 6314.
**Child's Play,**
112 Tooting High Street, SW17. Tel: 01-672 6470.
**Dolls House Toys,**
29 The Market, Covent Garden, WC2. Tel: 01-379 7243.
Also at 116 Lisson Grove, NW8. Tel: 01-723 1418.
**Domat Designs,**
41 Turnham Green Terrace, W4. Tel: 01-995 6618.
**Early Learning Centre,**
225 Kensington High Street, W8. Tel: 01-937 0419.

**Frog Hollow,**
15 Victoria Grove, W8. Tel: 01-584 5645.
**Hamleys,**
188 Regent Street, W1. Tel: 01-734 3161.
Largest toyshop in the world.
**James Galt,**
30 Great Marlborough Street, W1. Tel: 01-734 0829.
**Galt Toys,**
70 Fortis Green Road, N10. Tel: 01-444 0282.
**Knutz,**
1 Russell Street, Covent Garden, WC2. Tel: 01-836 3117.
**Kristin Baybars,**
3 Mansfield Road, NW3. Tel: 01-267 0934.
**Paddington and Friends,**
22 Crawford Place, W1. Tel: 01-262 1866.
**Playgear,**
3 Dennis Parade, Winchmore Hill Road, N14. Tel: 01-882 1293.
**Playthings,**
The Oxford Walk, 150/154 Oxford Street, W1. Tel: 01-580 5142.
**Pollock's Toy Theatres,**
44 The Market, Covent Garden, WC2. Tel: 01-379 7866.
**Raggity Ann's,**
26 Tranquil Vale, SE3. Tel: 01-852 7783.
**Rainbow,**
66 Fortune Green Road, NW6. Tel: 01-794 1616.
**Toy Town,**
193/5 Kentish Town Road, NW5. Tel: 01-485 8152.
**Tiger Tiger,**
219 King's Road, SW3. Tel: 01-352 8080.
**Tree House,**
237 Kensington High Street, W8. Tel: 01-937 7497.
**Tridias,**
6 Lichfield Terrace, Richmond, Surrey. Tel: 01-948 3459.
**Zebra Crossing,**
1 Salisbury Pavement, Dawes Road, SW6. Tel: 01-385 0824.

Most large department stores have a toy section:
**Harrods,**
Knightsbridge, SW1. Tel: 01-730 1234.

**Heal's,**
196 Tottenham Court Road, W1. Tel: 01-636 1666.
**Selfridges,**
Oxford Street, W1. Tel: 01-629 1234.

# 4

# Moving Around

## TRAVEL AND TRANSPORT

Don't be daunted by the thought of travelling round London with small children, even with a pushchair in tow. (For places to hire pushchairs see pages 68–9.) London Transport buses and underground services cater for every conceivable area, and this means easy access to places of interest that are further out of town. Under-5s travel free on buses and tubes. 5-year-olds and over either pay a flat fare (bus) or a graduated fare (tube) depending on the distance you travel. Check whether cheap day return tickets are available for your train journey.

**London Transport Headquarters,**
55 The Broadway, SW1 (St James's Park tube.) Tel: 01-222 1234.
24-hour telephone service. The enquiry offices will help you sort out any travel problems and also provide free maps and general tourist information. There are Travel Information Centres at the following tube stations:

Euston, Heathrow Central, King's Cross, Oxford Circus, Piccadilly Circus, St James's Park, Victoria.

# Information Services
## The London Tourist Board,
26 Grosvenor Gardens, SW1. Tel: 01-730 0791.
Give up-to-the minute details of what is happening in London.

Other Tourist Information Centres at:
## Victoria Station,
Opposite Platform 15. Open 8.00 am–10.30 pm.
## Selfridges,
Oxford Street, W1.
Ground floor. Open during normal shop hours.
## Harrods,
Knightsbridge, SW1.
4th floor. Open during normal shop hours.
## City of London Information Centre,
St Paul's Churchyard, EC4 (by St Paul's Cathedral). Tel: 01-606 3030.
Information on all events taking place in the City.
## Capital Radio's Helpline,
Tel: 01-388 7575. Open 9.00 am–5.30 pm Monday to Friday.
If you find yourself with a problem, whatever it might be, Capital's Helpline are the people to get in touch with. They provide valuable assistance and guidance covering all areas, for instance: how to find a solicitor; holiday insurance; the right speech for a wedding; general financial worries. These are only a few of the queries Helpline handles every day. If they can't answer a question straight away, they will put you in touch with someone who can. They also lend a sympathetic ear to personal problems that are often easier to talk about over the telephone. Charity and voluntary organizations have used Helpline to launch mini-appeals over the air. The response is always immediate and in the past they have managed to arrange such things as bicycles for a youth project and transport for a children's outing whose bus broke down at the last minute.
## Kidsline,
Studio D, Floral Hall, Covent Garden, WC2. Tel: 01-222 8070.
Kidsline have an enormous fund of information covering all aspects of children's London. Telephone lines are open 9.00 am–4.00 pm during half-term and holidays; 4.00–6.00 pm during term time Mondays to Fridays.

**Teledata,**
Tel: 01-200 0200.
Gives 24-hour information on where to locate emergency help, such as locksmiths, car breakdown services etc.

## Recorded Telephone Services

**Teletourist** have a 24-hour run-down on main events and places of interest in London. Tel: 01-246 8041 (in English); 01-246 8043 (in French); 01-246 8045 (in German).
**Children's London,**
Tel: 01-246 8007.
Weekly diary of children's events recorded by D.J. Ed "Stewpot" Stewart.
**Bedtime stories,**
Tel: 01-246 8000.
Different stories each night from 6.00 pm.
**Traffic Information Service,**
Tel: 01-246 8021.
It's useful if you plan to drive across London to telephone Traffic Information and avoid any traffic jams.
**Weather forecasts,**
Tel: 01-246 8091.

## Hire Shops for Pushchairs

There are a number of hire shops that rent out pushchairs. You leave a deposit and can hire by the day or week. Also check the telephone Yellow Pages.

**Hire Equipment,**
14 Queenstown Road, SW8. Tel: 01-622 3444.

**The Hire Shop,**

| | | |
|---|---|---|
| Acton | – | 183 Horn Lane, W3. Tel: 01-993 0792. |
| Fulham | – | 865 Fulham Road, SW6. Tel: 01-736 1769. |
| Hammersmith | – | 346 King Street, W6. Tel: 01-748 6740. |
| Hendon | – | 113 Brent Street, NW4. Tel: 01-202 7671 |
| Lewisham | – | Lewisham High Street, SE13. Tel: 01-690 7116. |

| | | |
|---|---|---|
| Leytonstone | – | 135 Leytonstone Road, E15. Tel: 01-555 0293. |
| Notting Hill | – | 192 Campden Hill Road, W8. Tel: 01-727 0897. |
| Richmond | – | 106 Sheen Road. Tel: 01-940 0112. |
| Shepherd's Bush | – | 14 The Vale, W3. Tel: 01-743 6300. |
| Stockwell | – | 282 Clapham Road, SW9. Tel: 01-720 6523. |
| Tooting | – | 190 Mitcham Road, SW17. Tel: 01-767 3127. |
| Tottenham | – | 451 High Road, N17. Tel: 01-801 3261. |

# OUT TO LUNCH

## Hamburgers

America came up with a cheap, speedy alternative to sitting down in restaurants – the hamburger. Now universally accepted, it has taken London in its stride and the problem of feeding small mouths on a day out has been solved and makes a welcome change from the regular crisps and sandwiches. There are now many more places to take children out to eat. Here are some you might like to visit:

**Burger King,**
25 Coventry Street, W1,
108 New Oxford Street, WC1,
146 Victoria Street, SW1,
13 Queensway, W2,
160 High Street, Hounslow, Middlesex.
**Great American Disaster,**
35 Haven Green, W5,
21 York Street, Twickenham, Middlesex.
**Hamburger Heaven,**
212 Edgware Road, W2,
159 Old Brompton Road, SW5,
29 Romilly Street, W1.
**Huckleberry's,**
425 Oxford Street, W1,
1a Tottenham Court Road, W1,
388 Uxbridge Road, W12,
679 Green Lanes, Wood Green, N22,
108 Queensway, W2.
**McDonald's,**
*North London:*
35 Golders Green Road, NW11,
295 Kentish Town Road, NW5,
13 Seven Sisters Road, N7,
31 Chase Side, Southgate, N14,
4 Harben Parade, Finchley Road, NW3,
6 Bank Buildings, Harlesden, NW10,
127 High Road, Kilburn, NW6,
99 High Road, Wood Green, N22,

*South London:*
159 Balham High Road, SW12,
90 Rushey Green, Catford, SE6,
30 St John's Road, Clapham Junction, SW11,
208 Earls Court Road, SW5,
55 Eltham High Street, SE9,
312 North End Road, SW6,
72 Rye Lane, Peckham SE15,
130 High Street, Penge, SE20,
121 Streatham High Road, SW16,
15 Westow Hill, Upper Norwood, SE19,
155 Victoria Street, SW1.
*East London:*
28 High Street North, Manor Park, E6,
258 Hoe Street, Walthamstow, E17.
*West London:*
122 Baker Street, W1,
178 Edgware Road, W2,
28 King's Mall, Hammersmith, W6,
57 Haymarket, W1,
108 Kensington High Street, W8,
1/4 Marble Arch, W1,
8 Oxford Street, W1,
310 Regent Street, W1,
65 Shaftesbury Avenue, W1,
88 Uxbridge Road, Shepherd's Bush, W12,
35 Strand, WC2,
134 Tottenham Court Road, W1,
147 High Street, Acton, W3.
*Middlesex:*
361 Station Road
124 High Street, Uxbridge,
62 High Street, Stains,
482 High Street, Wembley.

## Fish and Chips

Everyone has their "local", here are some others you might come across:

**Geale's Fish Restaurant,**
2/4 Farmer Street, W8.
**North Sea Fish Bar,**
8 Leigh Street, WC1.
**Shell Fish Bar,**
35 Lisson Grove, NW1.
**The Hungry Fisherman,**
46 Oxford Street, W1,
24 Thurloe Street, SW7,
142 Victoria Street, SW1.
**Staveley's,**
642 King's Road, SW6.

## Pizzas

Quite a number of pizza restaurants have opened in London.

**Pizza Huts** are excellent and extremely understanding in a crisis —
for instance if your toddler suddenly decides to redecorate the walls
with orange juice! They have high chairs for tiny children and
small seats for toddlers, and they even go to the trouble of providing crayons and paper. Branches at:
149 Earl's Court Road, SW5,
238 Kilburn High Road, NW6,
60 High Street, Hampstead, NW3,
67 Duke Street, W1,
39 New Broadway, Ealing, W5,
103 Queensway, W2,
198 Stamford Hill, N16,
114 Streatham Hill, SW2,
169 Upper Street, N1,
183 High Street, Wood Green, N22.
**Pizza Express,**
10 Dean Street, W1,
35 Earl's Court Road, W8,

30 Coptic Street, WC1,
15 Gloucester Road, SW7,
363 Fulham Road, SW10,
64 Heath Street, NW3,
20 Hill Street, Richmond, Surrey,
14 High Parade, High Road, Streatham, SW16,
84 High Street, Wimbledon, SW19,
189 New Kings Road, SW6,
26 Porchester Road, W2,
154 Victoria Street, SW1,
305 Upper Richmond Road, East Sheen, SW14,
137 Notting Hill Gate, W11.
**Pizza on the Park,**
11 Knightsbridge, Hyde Park Corner, SW1.
**Pizzaland,**
25 Argyll Street, W1,
187 Baker Street, W1,
58 Berwick Street, W1,
2a Castletown Road, W14,
44 Cranbourne Street, WC2,
64 Duke Street, W1,
204 Earl's Court Road, SW5,
227 Finchley Road, NW3,
70 Fleet Street, EC4,
75 Gloucester Road, SW7,
31 Haymarket, SW1,
46 High Street, Hampstead, NW3,
34 Hill Street, Richmond, Surrey,
80 King's Road, SW3,
14 Leicester Square, WC2,
15 New Burlington Street, W1,
20 Old Brompton Road, SW7,
10 Pembridge Road, W11,
101 Putney High Street, SW15,
78 Queensway, W2,
150 Southampton Row, WC1,
3 Wilton Road, SW1.

## Creperies
For something a little more unusual that might be fun to try:

**Asterix,**
329 King's Road, SW10.
**Obelix,**
294 Westbourne Grove, W11.
**The Creperie,**
56a South Molton Street, W1,
26 James Street, W1.

## Icecream
Speaks for itself, but Dayvilles are top of the league in quality, choice and sheer deliciousness. Here is a list of shops and restaurants selling Dayvilles icecream:

**Strikes,**
3a Baker Street, W1,
124 Southampton Row, WC1,
56 Edgware Road, W1,
144 Finchley Road, NW3,
9 Kensington High Street, W8,
1–2 Warwick Way, SW1,
103 Charing Cross Road, WC1.
**Dayvilles,**
126 Bayswater Road, W2,
490 Brixton Road, SW9,
18 The Broadway, Wood Green High Road, N22,
30 High Street, Richmond, Surrey,
10 Heath Street, NW3,
2 The Mall, Ealing, W5,
174 Muswell Hill Broadway, N10,
54 Golders Green Road, NW11,
62 Wimbledon Hill Road, SW19,
62 Gloucester Road, SW7,
85 Gloucester Road, SW7,
43–45 Haymarket, SW1.
**Marine Ices,**
8 Haverstock Hill, NW3.
**Mylo's Ice Cream,**
253 Chiswick High Road, W4.

## Department Stores
Don't forget that many of the big department stores have self-service restaurants and snack bars. There is also a **Happy Eater Family Restaurant** in Tottenham Court Road, W1 (Oxford Street end), with a special menu for small children (fish fingers and baked beans at half price), plus high chairs and "booster seats".

## Pubs with Gardens
For those times when you feel like a lunchtime drink and wish your local had a garden, here is a selection of pubs that do – and welcome children.

*North London:*
**Bird in Hand,**
100 Tottenhall Road, Palmers Green, N13.
**Five Bells,**
165/7 East End Road, Finchley, N2.
**Fox,**
413 Green Lanes, Wood Green, N13.
**Green Man,**
394 High Road, East Finchley, N2.
**Railway,**
5 Tottenham Lane, Horsney, N8.
**Rose & Crown,**
80 Church Street, Lower Edmonton, N9.
*North-West London:*
**Bird in Hand,**
12 West End Lane, NW6.
**Load of Hay,**
9 Brent Street (patio), NW4.
**Mannings,**
75 Brent Street, Hendon, NW4.
**Railway Tavern,**
129 Hale Lane, Edgware, NW7.
**Red Lion,**
253 Cricklewood Lane, NW2.
*South-West London:*
**Arab Boy,**
289 Upper Richmond Road, SW15.

**Bedford Park,**
233 Streatham High Road, SW16.
**Bridge Hotel,**
204 Castlenau, Barnes, SW13.
**Cottage,**
21 Colehill Lane, Fulham, SW6.
**Emma Hamilton,**
328 Kingston Road, Merton, SW20.
**Hollywood Arms,**
Hollywood Road, SW10.
**Jenny Lind,**
Inner Park Road, Wimbledon, SW19.
**Lass of Richmond Hill,**
8 Queens Road, Richmond, SW14.
**New Inn,**
345 Petersham Road, Ham Common, Richmond.
**Old Rose,**
22 Medway Street, SW1.
**Prince of Wales,**
14 Lillie Road, SW6.
**Telegraph,**
Telegraph Road, Putney Heath, SW15.
**Three Pigeons,**
87 Petersham Road, Richmond.
*South-East London:*
**Castle,**
179 Powis Street, Woolwich, SE18.
**Governor General,**
360 Verdant Lane, Catford, SE12.
**Lord Northbrook,**
116 Burnt Ash Road, Lee, SE12.
**Swiss Cottage,**
149 Stanstead Road, Forest Hill, SE23.
*East London:*
**Fir Trees,**
142 Hermon Hill, South Woodford, E18.
**Golden Fleece,**
166 Chapel Road, Manor Park, E12.

**Lord Raglan,**
199 Shernhall Street, Walthamstow, E17.
**Wakefield Arms,**
14 Park Road, Leyton, E10.
*West London:*
**Black Lion,**
2 South Black Lion Lane, W6.
**Crabtree,**
4 Rainville Road, W6.
**Feathers,**
Devonshire Road, W4.
**Hampshire Hog,**
227 King Street, W6.
**Hole in the Wall,**
12 Sutton Lane, W4.
**Queen of England,**
320 Goldhawk Road, W6.
**Queen's Head,**
13 Brook Green, W6.
**Raven,**
375 Goldhawk Road, W6.
**Red Lion**,
1 Waverton Street (forecourt), W1.
**Scarsdale,**
23a Edwardes Square, W8.

# 5

# Practical Help

## PROBLEMS AND EMERGENCIES

Here are some of the things you may need to know in order to make your time out in London potentially more trouble-free.

## Health

If you do not know anyone locally who can recommend a good doctor or dentist then the best plan is to contact your local town hall who will have up to date lists on file. They do not however recommend individual people. Libraries also have lists of doctors and dentists, and dentists are listed in the Yellow Pages directory under Dental Surgeons. It might be advisable to initiate your under-5 into making regular visits to the dentist as early as possible. Every six months is recommended and all dental treatment is free for children under 16.

### Health Clinics

To find out where your local health clinic is contact your district's Community Health Council (in telephone directory). Health clinics provide many services for under-5s, ranging from developmental checks (including injections against diphtheria, polio, etc.) to chiropody.

## The Community Health Council

The CHC is a statutory organization set up by the government to represent your interests in the health service. It will take note of any complaints or criticisms you might have and will give advice on all matters relating to health. Run by a cross-section of the public most of whom are voluntary members, it is a valuable "watch-dog", making sure that the service given to the public is the best. The CHC publicize widely in the local press, libraries, town halls and hospitals. To find your nearest centre consult the telephone directory or your local Citizens' Advice Bureau.

## The National Association for the Welfare of Children in Hospital,

7 Exton Street, SE1. Tel: 01-261 1738.

Each year over three-quarters of a million children are admitted to hospital. This can be a distressing experience not only for the child concerned but for parents as well. NAWCH provides a national information and counselling service to encourage and help parents to cope. It campaigns for all children to be nursed in children's wards with unrestricted visiting for parents, and accommodation for mothers who want to stay. Their groups all over the country provide the extra facilities needed such as hospital playgroups, mothers' beds and help with transport.

# Accidents

In case of accidents, dial 999 and ask for ambulance service or go to the casualty department of your nearest hospital. The following have 24-hour Accident and Emergency Departments.

*North-West Thames:*

**Barnet General Hospital,**
Wellhouse Lane, Barnet, Herts. Tel: 01-440 5111.

**Edgware General Hospital,**
Edgware, Middlesex. Tel: 01-952 2381.

**Central Middlesex Hospital,**
Acton Lane, Park Royal, NW10. Tel: 01-965 5733.

**Northwick Park Hospital,**
Watford Road, Harrow, Middlesex. Tel: 01-864 5311.

**West Middlesex Hospital,**
Twickenham Road, Middlesex. Tel: 01-560 2121.

**Ealing Hospital,**
Uxbridge Road, Southall, Middlesex. Tel: 01-574 2444.
**Royal Free Hospital,**
(teaching), Pond Street, NW3. Tel: 01-794 5000.
**Charing Cross Hospital,**
Fulham Palace Road, W6. Tel: 01-748 2040.
**Hammersmith Hospital,**
Du Cane Road, W12. Tel: 01-743 2030.
**Paddington Green Children's Hospital,**
Paddington Green, W2. Tel: 01-723 1081.
**St Mary's Hospital,**
Praed Street, W2. Tel: 01-262 1280.
**Middlesex Hospital,** '
Mortimer Street, W1. Tel: 01-636 8333.
**St Stephen's Hospital,**
Fulham Road, SW10. Tel: 01-352 8161.
**Westminster Hospital,**
Dean Ryle Street, SW1. Tel: 01-828 9811.
**Westminster Children's Hospital,**
Vincent Square, SW1. Tel: 01-828 9811.
*North-East Thames:*
**North Middlesex Hospital,**
Sterling Way, N18. Tel: 01-807 3071.
**London Hospital,**
(teaching), Whitechapel Road, E1. Tel: 01-247 5454.
**Hackney Hospital,**
Homerton High Street, E9. Tel: 01-985 5555.
**East Ham Memorial Hospital,**
Shrewsbury Road, E7. Tel: 01-472 3322.
**Whipps Cross Hospital,**
Whipps Cross Road, E11. Tel: 01-539 5522.
**Whittington Hospital,**
Highgate Hill, N19. Tel: 01-272 3070.
**University College Hospital,**
(teaching), Gower Street, WC1. Tel: 01-387 9300.
**St Bartholomew's Hospital,**
West Smithfield, EC1. Tel: 01-600 9000.
**Queen Elizabeth Hospital for Children,**
Hackney Road, E2. Tel: 01-739 8422.

*South-West Thames:*
**Queen Mary's Hospital,**
Roehampton Lane, SW15. Tel: 01-789 6611.
**St James' Hospital,**
Sarsfeld Road, SW12. Tel: 01-672 1222.
**St George's Hospital,**
Blackshaw Road, SW17. Tel: 01-672 1255.
*South-East Thames:*
**Greenwich District Hospital,**
Vanburgh Hill, SE10. Tel: 01-858 8141.
**Brook General Hospital,**
Shooters Hill Road, Woolwich, SE18. Tel: 01-856 5555.
**St Nicholas Hospital,**
Tewson Road, Plumstead, SE18. Tel: 01-854 2455.
**Lewisham Hospital,**
Lewisham High Street, SE13. Tel: 01-690 4311.
**Children's Hospital,**
321 Sydenham Road, SE26. Tel: 01-778 7031.
**Guy's Hospital,**
St Thomas Street, SE1. Tel: 01-407 7600.
**King's College Hospital,**
Denmark Hill, SE5. Tel: 01-274 6222.
**St Thomas' Hospital,**
Lambeth Palace Road, SE1. Tel: 01-928 9292.

There cannot be an absolute guarantee that a 24-hour service will always be maintained. In some instances, for special reasons and often at very short notice, it is sometimes necessary to close or partially close an accident and emergency department. In the unlikely event of this happening, the hospital would then arrange cover at another hospital, usually a neighbouring one.

## Teeth

For emergency dental treatment again contact your hospital's casualty department and they should be able to refer you to a dentist who is on call. Alternatively REDS (Radio Emergency Dental Service), a privately run 24-hour dental company, will be able to help you out at any time of the day or night. Ring 01-834 8345 giving your name and number and they will then get in touch with you and arrange treatment. Charges vary, so check when you telephone. The following hospitals specialize in dental treatment:

**Eastman Dental Hospital,**
256 Grays Inn Road, WC1. Tel: 01-837 7251.
**Royal Dental Hospital,**
32 Leicester Square, WC1. Tel: 01-930 8831.
**St George's Hospital,**
Tooting Grove, SW17. Tel: 01-672 1255.

## Eyes
**Moorfields Eye Hospital,**
High Holborn, WC1. Tel: 01-836 6611.
City Road, EC1. Tel: 01-253 3411.

## Late-Night Chemists
Doctors will advise on the rota for late-night chemists in your area. Police stations also keep a list of local emergency chemists and doctors.

**Boots,**
Piccadilly Circus, W1. Tel: 01-734 6126.
Open Monday to Friday 8.30 am–8.00 pm, Saturday 9.00 am–8.00 pm.
**Bliss,**
50–56 Willesden Lane, NW6. Tel: 01-624 8000.
Open 24 hours daily.
**John Bell and Croyden,**
50 Wigmore Street, W1. Tel: 01-935 5555.
Open Monday to Friday 9.00 am–6.00 pm. Dispensary 9.00 am–7.00 pm. Saturday 9.00 am–1.00 pm.
**Underwoods,**
75 Queensway, W2. Tel: 01-229 9266.
Open 9.00 am–10.00 pm. Sunday 10.00 am–10.00 pm.
114 Queensway, W2. Tel: 01-229 5126.
Open 9.00 am–10.00 pm. Sunday 10.00 am–10.00 pm.
60 King's Road, SW3. Tel: 01-589 3234.
Open 9.00 am–7.00 pm. Sunday 9.00 am–6.00 pm.
205 Brompton Road, SW3. Tel: 01-584 5391.
Open 9.00 am–7.00 pm. Late night Wednesday 9.00 am–8.00 pm. Sunday 10.00 am–6.00 pm.

**Warman Freed,**
45 Golders Green Road, NW11. Tel: 01-455 4351.
Open to midnight every night.

## Late-Night Food
In London shops that stay open late are more the exception than
the rule. Here are two that open their doors round the clock:
**24-hour Supermarket,**
68 Westbourne Grove, W2. Tel: 01-727 4927.
**Airey's Bargain Store,**
73 Willesden Lane, NW6. Tel: 01-624 5888.
Open 24 hours daily, except for a couple of hours between 8 and 10
pm on Mondays and Tuesdays.

## Late-Night Services
**Teledata,**
Tel: 01-200 0200.
2-hour information on emergency services such as plumbers, locksmiths, electricians, etc.

## Legal Advice
**Citizens' Advice Bureaux**
Offices are listed in phone directory, or call 01-379 6841 for details.
Offer free advice or can refer you to a solicitor.
**Law Centres**
For details of local centres which give free legal help, telephone
Law Centres Federation, 01-387 8570.
**Release,**
1 Elgin Avenue, W2.
Free legal service or can refer you to other organizations if
necessary. Open Monday, Tuesday, Friday 10.00 am–6 pm,
Wednesday 2.00–6.00 pm, Thursday 10.00 am–10.00 pm. For 24-
hour emergency service, telephone 01-603 8654.

## Lost Property
As well as the nearest police station, if relevant try:

**London Transport Lost Property Department,**
200 Baker Street, NW1.
Call in person to enquire about things lost on the underground or buses, or ask at the garage the bus came from. It may take a day or two for things to turn up, so check again if you're not successful straight away.

**Lost Property Office,**
15 Penton Street, N1.
For possessions left in London taxis.

## Money

**Chequepoint,**
37 Coventry Street, W1. Tel: 01-839 3772.
236 Earls Court Road, SW5. Tel: 01-270 3239.
Open 24 hours. Will cash cheques backed by a bank card.

# CHILDCARE

## Crèches

Crèches are a form of nursery where under-5s can be looked after while you do your own thing.

A growing number of Adult Education Institutes have some form of baby-minding facility for people attending their courses. If you would like to take advantage of this service get in touch with ILEA's Education Information Service, 01-633 1066, and they will send you a list of local AEIs that run crèches. Alternatively the magazine *Floodlight*, obtainable from W.H. Smiths, gives all the adult education institutes in the Greater London area. Check with each college individually to see what arrangements can be made.

There are four polytechnics that have crèche facilities:

**Polytechnic of Central London,**
309 Regent Street, W1. Tel: 01-580 2020.
**Polytechnic of North London,**
Holloway Road, N7. Tel: 01-607 2789.
**Polytechnic of South Bank,**
Borough Road, SE1. Tel: 01-928 8989.
**City of London Polytechnic,**
117 Houndsditch, EC3. Tel: 01-283 1030.

Colleges that have crèches:
**Brixton College of Further Education,**
56 Brixton Hill, SW2. Tel: 01-737 1166.
**Central Institute of Adult Education,**
Longford Street, NW1. Tel: 01-388 7106.
**North London College of Further Education,**
Camden Road, N7. Tel: 01-609 0041.
**Morley College,**
61 Westminster Bridge Road, SE1. Tel: 01-928 8501.
**Goldsmith College,**
Lewisham Way, SE14. Tel: 01-692 0211.
**South-East London College,**
Lewisham Way, SE4. Tel: 01-692 0353.
**Kingsway Princeton College,**
Sidmouth Street, WC1. Tel: 01-837 8185.

Several places mentioned in this book have crèche facilities enabling you to take advantage of the activities they offer:

**Battersea Arts Centre,**
Old Town Hall, Lavender Hill, SW11. Tel: 01-223 8413.
The centre is in the process of starting up a crèche. For more details telephone.

**Crofton Leisure Centre,**
Manwood Road, Crofton Park, SE4. Tel: 01-690 0273.
There are crèche facilities for the squash and badminton sessions held at the centre. Book before you go.

**Harrow Leisure Centre,**
Christchurch Avenue, Harrow, Middx. Tel: 01-863 5611.
If staff are available children of 3 years upwards will be looked after during the Ladies' Recreation sessions. Telephone for more details.

**Longridge Road Centre,**
46 Longridge Road, SW5. Tel: 01-370 6030.
A Thursday morning crèche for local residents only. Check for details.

**Sobell Sports Centre,**
Hornsey Road, N7. Tel: 01-607 1632.
Runs a Ladies' Programme twice a week which includes a crèche for children aged between 2 and 5 years (see page 53 for further details).

## Babysitters

Finding someone to babysit can be a problem wherever you live, especially if there isn't a convenient friend or relative close at hand. Try looking around for other mums and suggest taking turns babysitting for each other. Alternatively, school-leavers who have had experience in looking after younger brothers and sisters at home would no doubt welcome some extra money for babysitting. Your local shop might know of someone who babysits; inquire there, and check newsagents' windows for advertisements. If this doesn't work out and you don't know anyone who could pop in for the evening, there are babysitting agencies in London that can help. You pay for the service they provide and although it is an expensive way of going out (an agency fee is usually charged on top of wages), they can be useful in a crisis. (See also note on childminders on page 47.)

**Babyminders,**
67a Marylebone High Street, W1. Tel: 01-935 3515.
**Babysitters Unlimited,**
313 Brompton Road, SW3. Tel: 01-584 1046.
**Knightsbridge Nannies,**
5 Beauchamp Place, SW3. Tel: 01-584 9323.
**Problem Limited,**
44 Lupus Street, SW1. Tel: 01-828 8181.
**Universal Aunts Limited,**
36 Walpole Street, SW3. Tel: 01-730 9834.
**Solve Your Problem,**
25a Kensington Church Street, W8. Tel: 01-937 0906.

# INSTANT CATERING

## Quick-Cook Recipes

"And then there were four!" Have you ever been faced with the unexpected delight of three extra little faces for tea and wondered what on earth you were going to give them to eat? Here are a few helpful recipes, handed on to me by friends, which don't take long to prepare, won't clear out the larder and are sure-fire winners with children.

### SAVOURIES
### Egg Toast
Cut 4 slices of bread. Break 3 eggs into a bowl. Whisk. Coat bread in the egg mix until soggy. Place in oiled frying-pan and quickly fry. Tomato ketchup to garnish.
### Belted Bangers
4 strips of lasagne
8 oz. pork chippolatas
large can of tomato soup
level tsp. Worcestershire sauce
2 oz. Cheddar cheese – grated
½ oz. fresh bredcrumbs.
Cook lasagne in boiling water, salted, for 10 minutes. Drain and put to one side. Fry sausages until brown. Cut each piece of lasagne in half across and wrap each half round a chippolata. Place in oven-proof dish. Add the can of soup, Worcestershire sauce and salt and pepper together, and pour over sausages. Sprinkle cheese and breadcrumbs over soup. Bake at 200C (400F), mark 6, for 15–20 minutes. If soup is brought to the boil and the sausages are straight from the pan, the top can be crisped by popping quickly under a pre-heated grill.
### Cheese Dip
8 oz. Philly cheese
1 small grated carrot
1 small grated onion
1 desert spoon mayonnaise
salt and pepper.
Mix all the ingredients together. Dunk – raw carrots, mushrooms, cucumber, celery.

**Cheese and Ham**
12 slices of white bread
2 teaspoons chutney
6 thin slices of lean ham
6 oz. grated Cheddar cheese
butter and oil.
Butter the bread, then spread a little chutney on six of the slices.
Arrange the slices of ham over the chutney, sprinkle grated cheese
on top, then cover with buttered bread. Press the sandwiches
slightly to firm the filling, then cut each sandwich into two tri-
angles. Shallow fry in a little butter and oil over medium heat for
about 5 minutes on each side until the bread is golden crisp. Drain
well on kitchen paper and serve with a salad of tomatoes, mustard
and cress.

**Mixed Blessing**
Toast bread and cut into thick "soldiers". Top with mixture of
mashed sardines and grated cheese.

**Cheese and Tomato Pancakes**
The batter: 4 oz. plain flour, ¼ tsp. salt, 1 egg beaten, ½ pint
milk.
1 oz. butter for frying
4 tomatoes finely chopped
3 oz. grated cheese
3 oz. breadcrumbs
½ pint white sauce
salt and pepper.
Put flour and salt in a bowl. Add beaten egg and half milk. Beat
until smooth. Add the rest of the milk. Make 6 pancakes using
batter mixture. Fill each pancake with chopped tomatoes, grated
cheese and breadcrumbs. Fold in and place in an oven-proof dish.
Stir white sauce over pancakes and top with more grated cheese.
Place in oven for 20 minutes (190C, 375F, Gas Mark 5).

**SOMETHING SWEETER**
**Chocolate Crunchies**
Melt over a low heat 1 oz. margarine, 1 tsp. golden syrup. Take the
pan off the heat and add 2 oz. drinking chocolate, 3 oz. Rice
Crispies. Coat the Rice Crispies well with the mixture and then
spoon into paper cases or just leave to set in spoonfuls on a sheet of
kitchen foil.

## Butterfly Cakes

4 oz. butter or margarine
4 oz. castor sugar
4 oz. self-raising flour
1 large egg.

Cream butter and sugar until fluffy. Sift flour and beat the egg.
Fold in flour and egg mixture gradually. Place in paper cases and
bake in centre of oven at Gas Mark 4 for 30 minutes. When cool
remove a slice from the top of each. Fill hollows with butter cream,
then halve the removed tops and place them on top of the cakes like
wings.

## Raisin Cake

8 oz. self-raising flour
pinch of salt
6 oz. butter
4 oz. castor sugar
8 oz. raisins or sultanas
2 standard eggs.

Sift flour and salt into a bowl. Rub in the butter until the mixture
looks like breadcrumbs. Beat eggs lightly and add to dry
ingredients. Mix well and add about 4 tablespoons milk to make
moist. Mixture should drop from the spoon. Add fruit. Turn into a
tin and bake for 1¼ hours until golden brown. Gas Mark 5.

## Toffee Krispies

1 large tin Nestle's milk
3 oz. margarine
5 oz. granulated sugar
1 tablespoon golden syrup
2 oz. Rice Crispies.

Lightly grease a 7″-square tin. Melt margarine in a heavy sauce-
pan. Add sugar, milk and syrup. Heat gently stirring until the
sugar dissolves. Bring slowly to the boil and simmer for 20
minutes, stirring all the time. To test toffee, remove from heat and
drop a little into a cup of cold water. If it hardens, it's ready. Stir
in the Rice Crispies and pour quickly into prepared tin. When cool,
make into squares.

## Banana Bread

4½ oz. softened butter
2¼ oz. unsalted pecans or walnut halves
1½ oz. seedless raisins or mixed fruit
8 oz. plain flour
2½ teaspoons baking powder
¼ teaspoon ground nutmeg/cinnamon
½ teaspoon salt
½ teaspoon vanilla essence
1 egg
3½ oz. castor sugar.

Pre-heat oven to Mark 4 (350F). Spread ½ oz. of softened butter over the bottom of the bread tin. Reserve ¾ oz. nuts to garnish. Chop the rest coarsely and toss with fruit and 1 tablespoon flour. Sift the rest of the flour with the baking powder, nutmeg and salt. Peel the bananas and mash in a bowl until smooth. Stir in the vanilla. Cream the rest of the butter and sugar in a bowl until light and fluffy. Add the egg. When well blended, beat in the flour and bananas. Put the mixture in a bread tin and arrange the remaining nuts on top. Bake in the middle of the oven for 50–60 minutes (until knife comes out clean). Leave to cool.

## A BIT OF A SHAKE UP

The following recipes are good ways of disguising milk and giving it a bit of a zip.

### Chocana Shake

Put 2 chopped bananas, a smattering of orange peel, 3 tablespoons of drinking chocolate powder and ¾ pint of cold milk into a liquidizer – mix until frothy and foamy.

### Melon Shake

Take ½ a honeydew melon, ½ pint of milk, 1 egg, a dollop of vanilla icecream and put them into a liquidizer. Mix well.

### Icecream Dream

2 large spoons vanilla icecream, ½ pint cold custard, ¼ pint of cold milk and 1 egg. Blend it all together in a liquidizer until thick and creamy.

## Party advice

If the idea of giving a children's party fills you with horror, don't despair: help is at hand. Listed below are a number of agencies who will arrange everything for you.

**Catering for Kids,**
275 Dover House Road, SW15. Tel: 01-789 5161.
**The Children's Party Agency,**
32 Edge Street, W8. Tel: 01-727 8476.
**Smartie Artie,**
4 New Greens Avenue, St Albans, Herts. Tel: 0727 50837.
You supply the tea – they do the rest.

There is also a directory of professional puppeteers obtainable from **The Puppet Trust**, Battersea Arts Centre, Lavender Hill, SW11. Tel: 01-228 5335. It gives a comprehensive list of puppet companies that entertain at parties.

If you decide to do it all yourself *Giving a Children's Party* by Jane Cable-Alexander (St Michael) is an excellent book, full of helpful suggestions and useful tips.

For other ideas, call in at one of the shops that stock useful party paraphernalia such as jokes, magic tricks, masks, etc.
**Barnums,**
67 Hammersmith Road, W14. Tel: 01-602 1211.
**Knutz,**
1 Russell Street, WC2. Tel: 01-836 3117.
**Joker,**
97 Chiswick High Road, W4. Tel: 01-995 4118.
**Lewis Davenport,**
51 Great Russell Street, W1. Tel: 01-405 8524.
**Partymad,**
67 Gloucester Avenue, NW1. Tel: 01-586 0169.
**The Kensington Carnival Company,**
123 Ifield Road, SW10. Tel: 01-370 4358.
**Theatre Zoo,**
21 Earlham Street, WC2. Tel: 01-836 3150.

# GETTING DRESSED

## Clothing
Clothing that won't break the bank! (For other branches nearer your area telephone.)

**C & A,**
505 Oxford Street, W1. Tel: 01-629 7272.
Surprising range and quality here.
**British Home Stores,**
252 Oxford Street, W1. Tel: 01-629 2011.
A good choice of practical and inexpensive clothes.
**Littlewoods,**
508 Oxford Street, W1. Tel: 01-629 7840.
Very good choice of inexpensive clothes in their under-5 range.
**Marks and Spencer,**
458 Oxford Street, W1. Tel: 01-486 6151.
Great variety and excellent buys all round.
**Mothercare,**
461 Oxford Street, W1. Tel: 01-629 6621.
Everything for 5s and under including toys. All the clothes are practical, hard-wearing and reasonably priced.
**Laura Ashley,**
9 Harriet Street, SW1. Tel: 01-235 9797.
Pretty country coloured prints at reasonable prices.

There are also several smaller clothes shops that can be recommended:
**Benetton 012,**
129 Kensington High Street, W8. Tel: 01-937 3034.
Delicious clothes for diminutive trendies. Cords in palest peach, Viyella shirts in subtle checks. Italian chic at its best.
**Humla,**
235 Camden High Street, NW1. Tel: 01-267 7151.
Beautifully made hand-knits in bright cheery colours. Although basically a clothes shop they seem to have a bit of everything including books, toys, a playpen and a special area set aside for children to try out jigsaws, games etc.

**Little Horrors,**
16 Cheval Place, SW7. Tel: 01-589 5289.
10 William Street, SW1. Tel: 01-235 0531.
A good selection of French and Italian co-ordinates.
**Mother's Ruin,**
126 Holland Park Avenue, W11. Tel: 01-727 1116.
Splendid clothes for that special occasion but, as the name
suggests, they are not cheap. Shoes, toys and books are also on
sale.
**Pierrot,**
174 Wandsworth Bridge Road, SW6. Tel: 01-736 1123.
Not for the conventional, they have a marvellous selection of
padded jackets, flying suits and knickerbockers. Plus some lovely
Sun and Sand T-shirts and roll-necks in mouth-watering colours.
**Anthea Proud,**
61 South End Road, NW3. Tel: 01-435 0236.
Lovely Liberty-print dresses in cotton and Viyella as well as the
more casual kind of clothes. Good jeans and dungarees.
**Small Wonder,**
296 King's Road, SW3. Tel: 01-352 9608.
75 Heath Street, NW3. Tel: 01-794 3635.
A good range of French clothes and the more traditional type of
party clothes.
**Bright Sparks,**
3 The Lewisham Centre, SE13. Tel: 01-852 8869.
**Carolyn Brunn,**
211 Brompton Road, SW3. Tel: 01-584 1966.
**Bunters,**
84 Peckham High Street, SE15. Tel: 01-732 4989.
**The Children's Shop,**
23 Replingham Road, W18. Tel: 01-874 5988.
**Cockney Rebel,**
28 Westmoreland Road, W18. Tel: 01-701 9030.
**Hennes,**
481 Oxford Street, W1.
2 Kensington High Street, W8. Tel: 01-937 7825.

**Meeny's,**
241 King's Road, SW3. Tel: 01-351 4171.
197 Kensington High Street, W8. Tel: 01-937 7899.
163 Draycott Avenue, SW3. Tel: 01-581 2163.
**Tigermoth,**
166 Portobello Road, W11. Tel: 01-727 7564.

## Hand-me-Downs

An excellent hunting ground for useful bargains are the second-hand children's clothes shops that have opened recently. Children so often outgrow their clothes before they can possibly wear them out and the "nearly new" idea gives you an opportunity to find good clothes at rock-bottom prices. Enterprising young mums, not to be outdone by this new trend in children's clothes buying, have also taken up the idea, opening their doors once or twice a week from home. They all work on a simple sale-or-return basis. You take in the clothes you wish to sell, decide on a price (about half the original cost is usual), and your clothes are then put on sale. It is important to remember that clothes are more likely to be accepted if they are washed and ironed. Any items not sold will, after a period, be offered back to you or given to charity. The commission on clothes sold is between 30 and 50 per cent which works out as fair exchange for the work involved.

**Children's Bazaar,**
162c Sloane Street, SW1. Tel: 01-730 8901.
Open Monday to Friday 9.30 am–5.00 pm, Saturday 10.00 am–12.00 noon.
**Just Outgrown,**
28 Ramillies Road, W4. Tel: 01-995 4358.
Open Tuesday 9.30 am–3.00 pm and Thursday 9.30 am–5.00 pm.
**Second to None,**
10 Bassett Road, W10. Tel: 01-969 5872.
Open Tuesdays 9.30 am–4.30 pm.
**Small Change,**
Junction of Well Road and New End, NW3. Tel: 01-794 3043.
Open Tuesday to Friday 10.00 am–4.00 pm. Saturday 10.00 am–1.00 pm.

**Snips,**
19 Marlborough Road, W5. Tel: 01-567 4544.
Open Tuesdays 10.00 am–1.00 pm, Thursdays 10.00 am–4.00
pm. The first Saturday of the month 10.00 am–1.00 pm.
**Sunflower,**
18 Ellerker Gardens, Richmond Hill, Surrey. Tel: 01-940 8836.
Open Wednesdays 10.00 am–4.00 pm.
**Sign of the Times,**
17 Elystan Street, SW2. Tel: 01-589 4774.
Open Monday to Saturday 10.00 am–5.30 pm.
**Delphinium,**
68 Iffley Road, W6. Tel: 01-741 0120.
Open Tuesdays, Wednesdays, Fridays, Saturdays 10.00 am–3.00
pm. Late night Friday 10.00 am–6.00 pm.

## Shoes
Children's feet grow at an alarming rate, so make a point of going
to a good shoe shop at least once every three or four months to have
them measured professionally.Useful addresses:
**Children's Foot Health Register,**
Leather Trade House, 9 St Thomas Street, SE1. Tel: 01-407 5281.
Their useful guide lists shops which stock shoes in width fittings
and where trained staff will measure your child's feet carefully.
**The Society of Chiropodists,**
8 Wimpole Street, London W1. Tel: 01-580 3227.
Publishes an extremely good free leaflet on children's feet.
**Clark's Limited,**
Health Education, 40 High Street, Somerset, also publish helpful
leaflets.

## Hairdressers
Some West End salons cater for small children. Always ring and
make an appointment before you go.

**Barkers,**
Kensington High Street, W8. Tel: 01-937 5432.
2nd floor.

**D.H. Evans,**
Oxford Street, W1. Tel: 01-629 8800. 4th floor.
On Saturdays there is a stylist who is especially good with children's hair.
**Harrods,**
Knightsbridge, SW1. Tel: 01-730 1234.
The salon has a stylist who specializes in children's hair.
**John Lewis,**
Oxford Street, W1. Tel: 01-629 7711. 3rd floor.

# LAVATORIES

Have you ever been caught in the middle of a busy shopping spree
with a toddler in tow, not knowing where the nearest lavatories are?
Listed below is a selection of department stores in the West End
that might come in useful!

**John Barker,**
Kensington High Street, W8. 5th floor.
**British Home Stores,**
Kensington High Street, W8,
Lewisham, 156 High Street, SE15,
Wood Green, 26 High Road, N22.
All the above branches also have restaurants.
**Debenhams,**
Oxford Street, W1. 3rd floor.
**D.H. Evans,**
318 Oxford Street, W1. 5th floor.
**Fortnum & Mason,**
181 Piccadilly, W1. 1st floor and first-aid room on 2nd floor.
**Harrods,**
Knightsbridge, SW1. 1st floor and 4th floor mother-and-baby
rooms.
**Harvey Nichols,**
Knightsbridge, SW1. 3rd floor.
**Heal's,**
196 Tottenham Court Road, W1. 4th floor.
Pushchairs also available at front entrance to use in the shop.
**John Lewis,**
Oxford Street, W1. As well as lavatories there is a special room for
nappy changing 2nd floor.
**Littlewoods,**
Marble Arch, W1,
203–211 Oxford Street, W1,
King Street, W6.
All the above branches have restaurants.
**Selfridges,**
Oxford Street, W1. 3rd floor.
Also a mother and baby room.

# USEFUL ADDRESSES

## Specialized Help
### Gingerbread,
35 Wellington Street, WC2. Tel: 01-240 0953.
A nationally organized self-help association for one-parent families, where individuals who face particular problems can get together into a group and provide each other with mutual support.
### Invalid Children's Aid Association,
126 Buckingham Palace Road, SW1. Tel: 01-730 9891.
A registered charity running schools for handicapped children. In the Greater London area there are a number of social work officers dealing with the problems facing parents with handicapped children.
### The National Association for Gifted Children,
1 South Audley Street, W1. Tel: 01-499 1188/9.
Aims to help exceptionally gifted children and give support to parents, teachers and others concerned with their development.
### The National Children's Bureau,
8 Wakley Street, EC1. Tel: 01-278 9441.
An independent voluntary organization concerned with children's needs in the family, school, society in general. The Bureau sets out to make available any information there is about children, to improve liaison between people dealing with children and to evaluate and improve services and practice in childcare.
### The National Council for One-Parent Families,
255 Kentish Town Road, NW5. Tel: 01-267 1361.
Gives help to individual single parents through its Advice and Rights Department, which is staffed by professional qualified advisers, a welfare rights officer and legal officer. The service the council provides is free and confidential and inquiries are dealt with either by interview, letter or telephone.
### The National Deaf Children's Society,
45 Hereford Road, W2. Tel: 01-229 9272.
Helps deaf children break through the silence barrier and fights for a better education to suit their individual needs.
### National Society for Autistic Children,
1a Golders Green Road, NW11. Tel: 01-458 4376.
Provides and promotes day and residential centres for the care and

education of autistic children and helps parents by arranging meetings where they can exchange information.

**National Society for the Prevention of Cruelty to Children (NSPCC),**

1 Riding House Street, W1. Tel: 01-580 8812.

Works to prevent child abuse in all forms, to give practical help to families who are at risk and to encourage greater public awareness and understanding of child abuse.

**Royal National Institute for the Blind,**

224 Great Portland Street, W1. Tel: 01-388 1266.

Helps visually handicapped children and young people to take their place in society by supporting children in local schools as well as maintaining their own special schools.

**The Voluntary Council for Handicapped Children,**

8 Wakley Street, EC1. Tel: 01-278 9441.

Works under the aegis of the National Children's Bureau and is unique in providing a comprehensive service for all categories of handicap, giving help to both parents and professionals. Also produces a free booklet, *Help Starts Here,* and a series of fact sheets on various aspects of handicap.

# FREE PLACES

# INDEX

children's associations, 99–100
Children's Bazaar, 95
*Children's Book Bulletin,* 58
Children's Bookshop, 60
Children's Drama Workshop, 18
Children's Foot Health Register, 96
Children's Gallery (Science Museum), 44
Children's Hosital, 81
children's libraries, 57, 58, 101
Children's London (recorded service), 68
Children's Party Agency, 92
Children's Reference Library (National Book League), 58
Children's Shop, 94
Children's World, 60, 63
children's zoos, 28, 29, 35 (Battersea Park; Crystal Palace Park)
Child's Play, 63
chiropody, 78, 96
Chiswick Music Centre, 48
Chocana Shake (recipe), 91
Chocolate Crunchies (recipe), 89
cinemas, 17
circuses, 16
Citizens' Advice Bureaux, 79, 83
*City Farm News,* 31
city farms, 29–31
City Farms Advisory Service, 31
*City Limits,* 20
City of London Information

Centre, 67
City of London Polytechnic, 85
Clapham Baths, 54
Clapham Toy Library, 62
Clark's Limited, 96
climbing frames, 28, 37 (Ravenscourt Park), 39, 40
clinics, 78
Clissold Park, 35
clothes, 93–6; second-hand, 95–6
clowns, 14 (Lyric Theatre)
clubs and classes, 45
Cockney Rebel, 94
Collet's International Bookshop, 60
Collins Picture Lions, 58, 59
Common Stock Theatre, 14
Commonwealth Institute, 26, 101
Community Health Council, 79
Community Play Centre (toy library), 62
community theatre, 14
Concorde, 27
cooking, 88–91
Copthall Pool, 54
Coram Foundation for Children (toy library), 63
Coronation Coach, 25 (Royal Mews)
Cottage (pub), 76
cows, 29–30; mechanical, 26 (Commonwealth Institute)
Crabtree (pub), 77

# NOTES

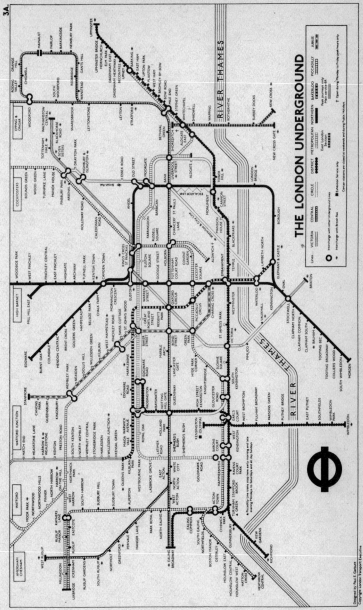

# THE LONDON UNDERGROUND

3A.

Designed by Paul E. Garbutt

Copyright London Transport Executive